Company's Coming ®

Garden Greens

Jean Paré

companyscoming.com
↑ visit our web-site

Front Cover Summer Crunch Salad,
page 45

Props Courtesy Of:
Anchor Hocking Canada
Canhome Global
Linens 'N Things

Back Cover

1. Spinach Squash
   Salad, page 48
2. Fruity Butter
   Lettuce Salad,
   page 75
3. Orange Butter
   Beans, page 135

Props Courtesy Of:
Linens 'N Things
The Bay
Winners Stores

*We gratefully acknowledge the following suppliers for their
generous support of our Test Kitchen and Photo Studio:*

Broil King Barbecues
Corelle ®
Lagostina ®
Tupperware ®

Garden Greens

First Printing May 2003

National Library of Canada Cataloguing in Publication

Paré, Jean
     Garden greens / Jean Paré.

(Original series)
Includes index.
ISBN 1-896891-54-3

     1. Cookery (Vegetables) 2. Salads. I. Title. II. Series: Paré, Jean.
Original series.

TX801.P37 2003   641.6'5   C2002-905676-4

Published by
COMPANY'S COMING PUBLISHING LIMITED
2311 - 96 Street
Edmonton, Alberta, Canada T6N 1G3
Tel: (780) 450-6223   Fax: (780) 450-1857
www.companyscoming.com

Company's Coming is a registered trademark owned by
Company's Coming Publishing Limited

Printed in Canada

Visit us on-line

companyscoming.com

| Who We Are | Browse Cookbooks | Cooking Tonight? | Home |

everyday ingredients

feature recipes

feature recipes — Cooking tonight? Check out this month's ***feature recipes***—absolutely FREE!

tips and tricks — Looking for some great kitchen helpers? ***tips and tricks*** are here to save the day!

reader circle — In search of answers to cooking or household questions? Do you have answers you'd like to share? Join the fun with ***reader circle***, our on-line question and answer bulletin board. Great for swapping recipes too!

cooking links — Other interesting and informative web-sites are just a click away with ***cooking links.***

cookbook search — Find cookbooks by title, description or food category using ***cookbook search***.

contact us — We want to hear from you—***contact us*** lets you offer suggestions for upcoming titles, or share your favourite recipes.

Company's Coming
COOKBOOKS®

Canada's
**most popular
cookbooks!**

Company's Coming Cookbook Series

Quick & easy recipes, everyday ingredients!

Original Series

- Softcover, 160 pages
- 6" x 9" (15 cm x 23 cm) format
- Lay-flat binding
- Full colour photos
- Nutrition information

Greatest Hits Series

- Softcover, 106 & 124 pages
- 8" x 9 9/16" (20 cm x 24 cm) format
- Paperback binding
- Full colour photos
- Nutrition information

Lifestyle Series

- Softcover, 160 pages
- 8" x 10" (20 cm x 25 cm) format
- Paperback & spiral binding
- Full colour photos
- Nutrition information

Special Occasion Series

- Hardcover & softcover, 192 pages
- 8 1/2" x 11" (22 cm x 28 cm) format
- Durable sewn binding
- Full colour throughout
- Nutrition information

See page 157
for a complete listing
of __all__ cookbooks
or visit
companyscoming.com

Table of Contents

The Company's Coming Story

Jean Paré grew up understanding that the combination of family, friends and home cooking is the essence of a good life. From her mother she learned to appreciate good cooking, while her father praised even her earliest attempts. When she left home she took with her many acquired family recipes, a love of cooking and an intriguing desire to read recipe books like novels!

"never share a recipe you wouldn't use yourself"

In 1963, when her four children had all reached school age, Jean volunteered to cater the 50th anniversary of the Vermilion School of Agriculture, now Lakeland College. Working out of her home, Jean prepared a dinner for over 1000 people which launched a flourishing catering operation that continued for over eighteen years. During that time she was provided with countless opportunities to test new ideas with immediate feedback—resulting in empty plates and contented customers! Whether preparing cocktail sandwiches for a house party or serving a hot meal for 1500 people, Jean Paré earned a reputation for good food, courteous service and reasonable prices.

"Why don't you write a cookbook?" Time and again, as requests for her recipes mounted, Jean was asked that question. Jean's response was to team up with her son, Grant Lovig, in the fall of 1980 to form Company's Coming Publishing Limited. April 14, 1981 marked the debut of "150 DELICIOUS SQUARES", the first Company's Coming cookbook in what soon would become Canada's most popular cookbook series.

Jean Paré's operation has grown steadily from the early days of working out of a spare bedroom in her home. Full-time staff includes marketing personnel located in major cities across Canada. Home Office is based in Edmonton, Alberta in a modern building constructed specially for the company.

Today the company distributes throughout Canada and the United States in addition to numerous overseas markets, all under the guidance of Jean's daughter, Gail Lovig. Best-sellers many times over in English, Company's Coming cookbooks have also been published in French and Spanish. Familiar and trusted in home kitchens around the world, Company's Coming cookbooks are offered in a variety of formats, including the original softcover series.

Jean Paré's approach to cooking has always called for quick and easy recipes using everyday ingredients. Even when travelling, she is constantly on the lookout for new ideas to share with her readers. At home, she can usually be found researching and writing recipes, or working in the company's test kitchen. Jean continues to gain new supporters by adhering to what she calls "the golden rule of cooking": never share a recipe you wouldn't use yourself. It's an approach that works— *millions of times over!*

Foreword

In recent years, salads have undergone a remarkable transformation. It used to be that salads were little more than a few lettuce leaves with a slice or two of tomato. Often the choice of reluctant dieters, salads were known for their low calorie and fat contents, as well as for their lack of flavour, colour, creativity and taste.

All of that has changed! Today's salads are still healthy but they are also fun, flavourful and versatile. In *Garden Greens*, you will find many recipes for salads that are savoury, warm, chilled, fresh, tossed, marinated, spicy, mild, light and rich. They may include fresh or dried fruits, vegetables, grains, cheeses, eggs, pasta, seafood, nuts, olives, fresh herbs and much, much more. Salads today are limited only by your imagination!

Salads are not only delicious and nutritious, they can be served and made in a variety of unique ways. *Garden Greens* is brimming with new and creative ideas. You will find a few traditional salad recipes as well as many others calling for more creative and exotic greens. Salads can be a delightful starter to a sit-down dinner, a palate cleanser between courses, the perfect selection for a light lunch or a satisfying main dish made with a variety of hearty ingredients. They can even be served at the end of a meal, European-style. Adding to the versatility of salads, they can easily be made ahead of time and served buffet-style to a crowd, made in large quantities and kept in the refrigerator for several days or made one dish at a time for a personal touch.

Garden Greens has a number of recipes for delicious vegetable side dishes to complement and enhance any main dish. These recipes incorporate a wide variety of vegetables (green, of course) to add colour, crunch and flavour to your meals.

Few things are more comforting than a bowl of homemade soup created from the freshest ingredients. So we have included some attractive, palate-pleasing soup recipes that are sure to liven up any table. The addition of fresh garden greens creates vibrant flavours your guests will long remember!

With *Garden Greens*, you can welcome a new generation of sensational salads, side dishes and soups into your home. Your old lettuce and tomato salad of years gone by will be green with envy!

Jean Paré

Each recipe has been analyzed using the most up-to-date version of the Canadian Nutrient File from Health Canada, which is based on the United States Department of Agriculture (USDA) Nutrient Data Base. If more that one ingredient is listed (such as "hard margarine or butter"), the first ingredient is used in the analysis. Where an ingredient reads "sprinkle," "optional," or "for garnish," it is not included as part of the nutrition information.

Margaret Ng, B.Sc. (Hon), M.A.
Registered Dietitian

Glossary

Arugula (ah-ROO-guh-lah): A herbaceous plant with tender, green, irregularly shaped leaves and a distinct peppery flavour. Often served with other greens. Place the roots in a glass of water and refrigerate for up to three days.

Belgian Endive (EN-dyv): Also known as witloof, meaning "white leaf." A vegetable with a small, tightly packed, cigar-shaped head of creamy white or red leaves. Soaking and washing are not recommended; simply wipe the outer leaves with a damp cloth. Prepare at the last minute, as it will darken and become more bitter when exposed to air. Refrigerate, wrapped loosely in a damp paper towel and placed in a paper bag, for up to two days.

Bibb Lettuce: A vegetable plant that is a member of the butterhead family. The leaves have a soft, buttery texture, a mild, delicate flavour and are slightly smaller than butter lettuce leaves. Some varieties have a reddish tinge. (See Butter Lettuce for storage information.)

Bok Choy (bahk CHOY): A type of cabbage with a mild flavour. Has veiny, dark green leaves and white ribs, with the exception of Shanghai bok choy, which has tender, light green ribs and leaves. Baby bok choy is a smaller version of the main variety and is often sold in bunches. Can be substituted in recipes calling for cabbage, spinach or chard. Refrigerate in a perforated plastic bag for up to three days.

Butter Lettuce: Also called Bibb or Boston lettuce. A vegetable plant that grows in small, round, loosely formed heads. The pale green leaves are tender and have a luscious, sweet quality. Wash gently. Refrigerate, wrapped loosely in a damp paper towel or placed in an airtight container, for up to three days.

Chinese Broccoli: Also known as gai-lohn. A type of broccoli with longer stems and wider leaves. The leaves are ragged around the edge and are blue-green in colour. Known for its very delicate flavour. Refrigerate in a perforated plastic bag for up to three days.

Curly Endive (EN-dyv): An annual plant. Grows in loose heads with green outer leaves that curl at the tips. Has a prickly texture and a mild, slightly bitter flavour. Refrigerate in a perforated plastic bag for up to five days.

Fennel: A vegetable with pale green, celery-like stems and bright green leaves growing out of a bulbous base. Has a slightly sweet licorice flavour that becomes extremely mild when cooked. Refrigerate in a perforated plastic bag for about one week.

Fiddleheads: Tightly coiled, bright green fern shoots with a mild flavour. Purchase firm shoots with brown scales. Trim the ends just before serving. Refrigerate, wrapped in a paper towel and placed in a paper bag, for up to two days.

Green Leaf Lettuce: A vegetable plant with curly, tender leaves that do not grow in a head. They are long and broad, range in colour from green to reddish-green and have a mild hazelnut flavour. Refrigerate, wrapped loosely in a damp paper towel or placed in an airtight container, for up to three days.

Iceberg Lettuce: Also known as head lettuce. A vegetable plant that grows in crisp, round, tightly packed heads. Its pale green leaves are fairly wilt-resistant and have a very neutral flavour. Purchase heads with no signs of browning that feel solid when squeezed. Refrigerate, wrapped loosely in a damp paper towel or placed in an airtight container, for up to two weeks.

Leek: A vegetable with a thick, cylindrical stalk. Has a sweeter, milder flavour than an onion. The white, tender part of the stalk that grows underground is most commonly used. To prepare, trim rootlets and leaf ends, slice from top to within 3/4 inch (2 cm) of bottom and wash thoroughly. Refrigerate in a perforated plastic bag for up to one week.

Mixed Salad Greens: Called mesclun by the French. A mix of small, young salad greens. The mix varies but often includes arugula, curly endive, mizuna, oak leaf, radicchio and sorrel. Buy in bags or create your own mix. Refrigerate in a perforated plastic bag for up to five days.

Okra (OH-kruh): The fruit of a vegetable plant. A bright green, tapered pod with a thin, edible skin and edible seeds. Has a mild flavour similar to that of eggplant. Releases a sticky substance when cut that can be used as a thickening agent. Purchase firm pods that are less than 4 inches (10 cm) long. Refrigerate in a paper bag for up to three days.

Pea Sprouts: Taste like fresh peas and are bright green in colour. Eat raw or briefly cooked. Rinse daily under cold water to extend their life. Wrap the roots in a damp paper towel and refrigerate for about one week.

Radicchio (rah-DEE-kee-oh): A garden plant ranging in colour from reddish-green to bright red with white veins. The leaves are round and firm with a tart, slightly bitter flavour. Refrigerate in a perforated plastic bag for up to one week.

Rapini (rah-PEE-nee): A vegetable that is also known as broccoli raab, rabe or Italian broccoli. Grows in thin green stalks with tiny, broccoli-like clusters. The entire plant is edible. Has a slightly bitter flavour. The stalks are milder in flavour than the leaves. Refrigerate in a perforated plastic bag for about one week.

Romaine (roh-MAYN) Lettuce: A vegetable plant with long, crisp, deep green leaves and a slightly bitter flavour. A popular choice for Caesar salads. Avoid heads with soft, dull-looking leaves that have any browning on the edges. Refrigerate, wrapped loosely in a damp paper towel or placed in an airtight container, for up to five days.

Ruby Chard: A plant similar to Swiss chard but with bright red stalks and dark, greenish-red leaves. Slightly stronger in flavour than spinach. Refrigerate in a perforated plastic bag for up to four days.

Snow Pea Pods: Bright green, sweet pea pods that are entirely edible. Purchase flat, crisp pods with barely developed seeds. Eat raw or briefly cooked. Pinch off the tips before serving. Refrigerate in a perforated plastic bag for up to four days.

Spinach: A vegetable plant with dark green leaves that may be either curly or smooth. Can be purchased frozen, canned or fresh.

Has a slightly bitter flavour. Refrigerate fresh spinach in a perforated plastic bag for up to five days.

Suey Choy: Also called Chinese cabbage or napa cabbage. A plant with pale green, thickly veined leaves which are broad and compact. Their high water content makes them crisp and refreshing. Milder in flavour than head cabbage. Refrigerate in a perforated plastic bag for up to two weeks.

Sugar Snap Pea Pods: A cross between the English pea and the snow pea, these pea pods are sweet and completely edible. Purchase plump, crisp pods with a vibrant green colour. Eat raw or briefly cooked. Refrigerate in a perforated plastic bag for up to four days.

Swiss Chard: A plant with crinkly leaves and long, celery-like stalks. The leaves are milder than spinach leaves but the two are relatively interchangeable. The stems should be prepared like celery. Refrigerate in a perforated plastic bag for up to four days.

Watercress: An aquatic plant with thin, crisp stalks and small, glossy, dark green leaves. Has a slightly bitter, peppery flavour. Often sold in small bunches. Place the stalks in a glass of water, cover with a plastic bag and refrigerate for up to two days.

Glossary

Creamy Balsamic Romaine Hearts

This beautiful salad has crisp romaine heart wedges mixed with fresh vegetables and ham. The dressing tops it all off for an elegant presentation.

Small romaine lettuce hearts, quartered	2	2
Halved cherry tomatoes	2 cups	500 mL
Thinly sliced red onion	1/3 cup	75 mL
Grated Parmesan cheese	1/3 cup	75 mL
Paper-thin prosciutto (or deli) ham slices, cooked crisp and coarsely crumbled	1 – 2 oz.	28 – 57 g
CREAMY BALSAMIC DRESSING		
Half-and-half cream (or milk)	1/4 cup	60 mL
Sour cream	1/4 cup	60 mL
Balsamic vinegar	1/4 cup	60 mL
Garlic clove, minced (or 1/4 tsp., 1 mL, powder)	1	1
Salt	1/4 tsp.	1 mL
Coarsely ground pepper (or 1/8 tsp., 0.5 mL, pepper)	1/4 tsp.	1 mL

Divide lettuce quarters among 4 individual salad plates.

Arrange next 4 ingredients around lettuce.

Creamy Balsamic Dressing: Put all 6 ingredients into small bowl. Stir until well combined. Makes about 3/4 cup (175 mL) dressing. Drizzle over vegetable mixture. Serves 4.

1 serving: 176 Calories; 10.5 g Total Fat (3.6 g Mono, 0.9 g Poly, 5.3 g Sat); 24 mg Cholesterol; 12 g Carbohydrate; 4 g Fibre; 11 g Protein; 458 mg Sodium

Pictured on page 72.

Individual Bistro Salads

*The crunchy romaine and peppery watercress are
complemented by a fresh lemony dressing.*

LEMON GARLIC DRESSING		
Olive (or cooking) oil	1/4 cup	60 mL
Lemon juice	3 tbsp.	50 mL
Garlic cloves (or 1/2 tsp., 2 mL, powder)	2	2
Finely grated lemon zest	1 tsp.	5 mL
Salt	1/4 tsp.	1 mL
Cut or torn romaine lettuce, lightly packed	4 cups	1 L
Trimmed watercress	2 cups	500 mL
Golden Delicious apple (with peel)	1	1
Medium avocado	1	1
Slices of Havarti cheese (about 4 oz., 113 g), cut in half diagonally	4	4
Chopped fresh parsley (or 1/2 tsp., 2 mL, flakes)	2 tsp.	10 mL
Chopped fresh chives (or 1/2 tsp., 2 mL, dried)	2 tsp.	10 mL
Sunflower seeds, toasted (see Tip, page 86)	2 tsp.	10 mL
Chopped walnuts, toasted (see Tip, page 86)	2 tsp.	10 mL

Lemon Garlic Dressing: Process first 5 ingredients in blender until smooth.
Let stand for 30 minutes to blend flavours. Makes 1/2 cup (125 mL) dressing.

Toss lettuce and watercress in medium bowl. Arrange on 4 individual
salad plates.

Just before serving, core apple. Slice into thin wedges.

Cut avocado in half lengthwise. Discard pit. Carefully scoop flesh out,
trying to keep intact. Cut lengthwise into 1/4 inch (6 mm) slices. Arrange
apple, avocado and cheese over lettuce mixture. Drizzle each serving with
2 tbsp. (30 mL) dressing.

Combine remaining 4 ingredients in small bowl. Divide and sprinkle over
each serving. Serves 4.

*1 serving: 358 Calories; 31.3 g Total Fat (17.8 g Mono, 3.5 g Poly, 8.1 g Sat); 29 mg Cholesterol;
13 g Carbohydrate; 4 g Fibre; 10 g Protein; 379 mg Sodium*

Cucumber Avocado Salad

An attractive, rich-tasting salad with an intense combination of flavours. This would be perfect for brunch or lunch and would go well with an omelet or quiche.

English cucumber (with peel), sliced on diagonal	1	1
Red pepper, thinly sliced	1	1
Large avocados, sliced	2	2
Smoked salmon, thinly sliced	4 oz.	113 g
CREAMY LEMON DRESSING		
Sour cream	3 tbsp.	50 mL
Water	2 tbsp.	30 mL
Chopped fresh dill (or 3/4 tsp., 4 mL, dill weed)	1 tbsp.	15 mL
Lemon juice	1 tbsp.	15 mL
Salt	1/4 tsp.	1 mL
Finely chopped red onion	1/4 cup	60 mL
Coarsely chopped capers (optional)	1 tbsp.	15 mL
Coarsely ground pepper, sprinkle		

Arrange cucumber, red pepper, avocado and salmon on 4 individual salad plates.

Creamy Lemon Dressing: Combine first 5 ingredients in small bowl. Makes about 1/3 cup (75 mL) dressing. Drizzle over cucumber mixture.

Sprinkle with onion, capers and pepper in order given. Serves 4.

1 serving: 271 Calories; 21.4 g Total Fat (12.6 g Mono, 2.8 g Poly, 4.2 g Sat); 11 mg Cholesterol; 16 g Carbohydrate; 4 g Fibre; 9 g Protein; 390 mg Sodium

Pictured on page 89.

Coleslaw With Shrimp Crisps

An interesting, very tasty coleslaw salad with thin, delicious Shrimp Crisps.
The crisps can be made ahead, chilled and then reheated if desired.

SHRIMP CRISPS

Raw medium shrimp (fresh or frozen, thawed), peeled and deveined	8 oz.	225 g
Cornstarch	1 tbsp.	15 mL
Green curry paste	1 tsp.	5 mL
Finely grated peeled gingerroot	1/2 tsp.	2 mL
Garlic clove, minced (or 1/4 tsp., 1 mL, powder)	1	1
Salt	1/4 tsp.	1 mL
Rice paper rounds (9 inch, 22 cm, size)	5	5
Cooking oil, for deep-frying		

COCONUT DRESSING

Evaporated milk (not skim)	1/2 cup	125 mL
Medium coconut	1/4 cup	60 mL
Mayonnaise (not salad dressing)	2 tbsp.	30 mL
Sweet (or regular) chili sauce	1 tbsp.	15 mL
Lime juice	2 tsp.	10 mL
Golden corn syrup	1 tsp.	5 mL
Celery seed	1/4 tsp.	1 mL
Salt	1/2 tsp.	2 mL
Finely shredded green cabbage, lightly packed	3 cups	750 mL
Green onions, cut crosswise into 2 inch (5 cm) pieces	2	2
Medium carrot, cut julienne	1	1
Coconut ribbons, toasted (see Tip, page 86), for garnish		

Shrimp Crisps: Process first 6 ingredients in blender until smooth.

Spread each rice paper round with about 2 tbsp. (30 mL) shrimp mixture. Cut into quarters with scissors.

(continued on next page)

Deep-fry, shrimp-side down, in hot (375°F, 190°C) cooking oil for about 1 1/2 minutes, turning once, until golden. Remove to paper towels to drain.

Coconut Dressing: Put evaporated milk and coconut into small saucepan. Bring to a boil on medium. Boil for 3 minutes, stirring frequently. Remove from heat. Cool to room temperature.

Add next 6 ingredients. Stir until smooth. Chill. Makes 2/3 cup (150 mL) dressing.

Put cabbage, green onion and carrot into large bowl. Drizzle with dressing. Toss. Arrange on 4 individual salad plates. Divide and arrange crisps around each salad.

Scatter with coconut ribbons. Serves 4.

1 serving: 333 Calories; 20.9 g Total Fat (8.4 g Mono, 4.5 g Poly, 6.8 g Sat); 99 mg Cholesterol; 22 g Carbohydrate; 2 g Fibre; 16 g Protein; 681 mg Sodium

Pictured on page 108.

Brie And Apple Salad

This salad is fresh, flavourful and light. The tartness of the apple is mellowed by the creamy Brie cheese.

Mixed salad greens	4 cups	1 L
Red apple (not Delicious), with peel, cored and thinly sliced	1	1
Brie cheese, thinly sliced	4 oz.	113 g
MUSTARD DRESSING		
Whipping cream	1/4 cup	60 mL
Lemon juice	1 tbsp.	15 mL
Grainy mustard	1 tbsp.	15 mL
Maple (or maple-flavoured) syrup	1 tbsp.	15 mL
Salt	1/4 tsp.	1 mL

Arrange salad greens on 4 individual salad plates.

Top with apple and cheese.

Mustard Dressing: Put all 5 ingredients into small bowl. Stir until well combined. Makes about 1/2 cup (125 mL) dressing. Drizzle over salad green mixture. Serves 4.

1 serving: 197 Calories; 13.7 g Total Fat (3.8 g Mono, 0.6 g Poly, 8.2 g Sat); 47 mg Cholesterol; 13 g Carbohydrate; 1 g Fibre; 8 g Protein; 407 mg Sodium

Grape Spinach Salad

Fresh strawberries and grapes add colour and sweetness to this salad.
The addition of poppy seeds to the dressing creates a unique flavour and texture.

Spinach, stems removed, lightly packed	4 cups	1 L
Sliced fresh strawberries	1 cup	250 mL
Seedless green grapes, halved	1/2 cup	125 mL
Seedless red grapes, halved	1/2 cup	125 mL
Sunflower seeds, toasted (see Tip, page 86)	1/4 cup	60 mL
POPPY SEED DRESSING		
Peanut (or cooking) oil	2 tbsp.	30 mL
Balsamic vinegar	2 tbsp.	30 mL
Maple (or maple-flavoured) syrup	1 tbsp.	15 mL
Poppy seeds	1 tbsp.	15 mL
Salt	1/4 tsp.	1 mL

Arrange spinach on 4 individual salad plates.

Top with strawberries, green and red grapes and sunflower seeds.

Poppy Seed Dressing: Combine all 5 ingredients in jar with tight-fitting lid. Shake well. Makes 1/3 cup (75 mL) dressing. Drizzle over spinach mixture. Serves 4.

1 serving: 183 Calories; 13.4 g Total Fat (4.3 g Mono, 6.4 g Poly, 1.9 g Sat); 0 mg Cholesterol; 15 g Carbohydrate; 3 g Fibre; 4 g Protein; 197 mg Sodium

Pictured on page 17.

1. Grape Spinach Salad, above
2. Pepper Mango Salsa, page 133
3. Papaya And Mixed Greens, page 23

Props Courtesy Of: Wiltshire®

Arranged Salads

Lima Bean Salad

A high-protein salad with the unique addition of lima beans.
Small or medium beans work best in this recipe. The sweet,
creamy dressing mellows out the spicy kick of the peppers.

Can of lima beans, rinsed and drained	19 oz.	540 mL
Chopped celery	1 1/2 cups	375 mL
Hard-boiled eggs, sliced (reserve 6 slices for garnish)	2	2
Finely chopped sweet (or red) onion	2 tbsp.	30 mL
Finely chopped pickled jalapeño pepper (optional)	1 tbsp.	15 mL
CREAMY DRESSING		
Salad dressing (or mayonnaise)	1/3 cup	75 mL
Sweet pickle relish	2 tbsp.	30 mL
Milk	2 tsp.	10 mL
Salt	1/4 tsp.	1 mL
Shredded romaine lettuce, lightly packed	4 1/2 cups	1.1 L

Put first 5 ingredients into medium bowl. Toss gently.

Creamy Dressing: Combine first 4 ingredients in small bowl. Makes 1/2 cup (125 mL) dressing. Drizzle over bean mixture. Toss.

Arrange lettuce on 6 individual salad plates. Top with bean mixture. Garnish with reserved egg slices. Serves 6.

1 serving: 170 Calories; 8.8 g Total Fat (4.5 g Mono, 2.6 g Poly, 1.1 g Sat); 75 mg Cholesterol; 16 g Carbohydrate; 1 g Fibre; 7 g Protein; 383 mg Sodium

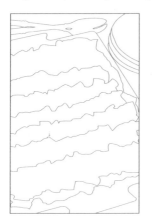

Lined-Up Salad, page 26

Props Courtesy Of: Pfaltzgraff Canada

Lettuce Wedges Salad

A well-dressed arranged salad with crisp lettuce and simple, yet elegant, toppings.

CREAMY VEGETABLE DRESSING

Half-and-half cream (or homogenized milk)	1/3 cup	75 mL
Coarsely chopped green pepper	1/4 cup	60 mL
Coarsely chopped carrot	2 tbsp.	30 mL
Garlic clove (or 1/4 tsp., 1 mL, powder)	1	1
Green onion, sliced	1	1
Lemon juice	1 tbsp.	15 mL
Worcestershire sauce	1/2 tsp.	2 mL
Granulated sugar	1/2 tsp.	2 mL
Salt	1/4 tsp.	1 mL
Dried crushed chilies	1/4 tsp.	1 mL
Coarsely ground pepper, heavy sprinkle		
Mayonnaise	3/4 cup	175 mL
Head of iceberg lettuce	1	1
Slices of English cucumber (with peel)	18	18
Finely shredded red cabbage	1/2 cup	125 mL
Cherry tomatoes	18	18

Creamy Vegetable Dressing: Process first 11 ingredients in blender until almost smooth.

Add mayonnaise. Process until well blended. Chill for 30 minutes to blend flavours. Makes 1 1/2 cups (375 mL) dressing.

Cut out root end of lettuce head with sharp knife. Discard. Rinse lettuce under cold water. Let stand in colander for 10 minutes to drain. Place folded paper towels under cut end and transfer to resealable freezer bag. Chill for about 3 hours to allow lettuce to crisp. Remove and discard soft outer leaves. Carefully cut head into 6 wedges, keeping wedges intact as best as possible. Drizzle chilled individual salad plates with about 2 tbsp. (30 mL) dressing each. Place lettuce wedge on each plate, fanning slightly.

Arrange cucumber, red cabbage and tomatoes decoratively on each plate. Drizzle with remaining dressing. Serves 6.

1 serving: 261 Calories; 25.2 g Total Fat (13.4 g Mono, 8 g Poly, 3.2 g Sat); 22 mg Cholesterol; 7 g Carbohydrate; 1 g Fibre; 3 g Protein; 277 mg Sodium

Pictured on page 126.

Goat Cheese Cranberry Salad

A unique salad with vibrant red berries and crisp, golden deep-fried cheese.
The thick dressing adds a subtle tang to the overall flavour.

Large egg	1	1
Fresh bread crumbs	1 cup	250 mL
Goat (chèvre) cheese, cut into 1/4 inch (6 mm) thick slices	8 oz.	225 g
Cooking oil, for deep-frying		
Cut or torn butter lettuce	4 cups	1 L
Dried cranberries	6 tbsp.	100 mL
APPLE C		
Olive (o	3 tbsp.	50 mL
Apple cid	2 tbsp.	30 mL
Cranberry	2 tbsp.	30 mL
Grainy mu	1 tbsp.	15 mL
Salt	1/4 tsp.	1 mL
Pepper, j		

Beat egg   ace bread crumbs in separate shallow
dish or or   heese slices. Dip remaining cheese
slices into   rumbs until well coated.

Deep-fry,   90°C) cooking oil for 2 to 3 minutes
until gold   s to drain.

Arrange le   individual salad plates. Top with
deep-fried   cheese slices. Sprinkle over top.

Apple Cid   ingredients in jar with tight-fitting
lid. Shake   nL) dressing. Drizzle over lettuce
mixture. Serves 6.

1 serving: 356 Calories; 24.8 g Total Fat (11.1 g Mono, 2.8 g Poly, 9.5 g Sat); 66 mg Cholesterol; 22 g Carbohydrate; 2 g Fibre; 12 g Protein; 505 mg Sodium

Crispy Lentil Ball Salad

A nice change from the ordinary! This salad is topped with delicious, deep-fried lentil balls. Their warm, spicy cornmeal coating is perfectly complemented by the sweet, tangy dressing.

Red lentils	2/3 cup	150 mL
Water, to cover		
Chopped green onion	3 tbsp.	50 mL
Garlic cloves, halved (or 1/2 tsp., 2 mL, powder)	2	2
Chopped green pepper	1/3 cup	75 mL
Curry powder	2 tsp.	10 mL
Fresh bread crumbs	1 2/3 cups	400 mL
Salt	1/2 tsp.	2 mL
Grated medium Cheddar cheese	2/3 cup	150 mL
Grated zucchini (with peel)	1/2 cup	125 mL
Yellow cornmeal	1/2 cup	125 mL
Cooking oil, for deep-frying		
Mixed salad greens	8 cups	2 L
Thinly sliced red onion	2/3 cup	150 mL
PARSLEY DRESSING		
Cooking oil	3 tbsp.	50 mL
Coarsely chopped fresh parsley (or 2 1/4 tsp., 11 mL, flakes)	3 tbsp.	50 mL
Coarsely chopped fresh mint leaves (or 2 1/4 tsp., 11 mL, dried)	3 tbsp.	50 mL
Plain yogurt (not low-fat or non-fat)	1/3 cup	75 mL
White wine vinegar	3 tbsp.	50 mL
Liquid honey	3 tbsp.	50 mL
Garlic clove, halved (or 1/4 tsp., 1 mL, powder)	1	1
Salt	1/4 tsp.	1 mL

Cover lentils with water in medium saucepan. Bring to a boil. Reduce heat to medium-low. Cover. Cook for about 10 minutes until tender. Drain.

Put 1/2 of lentils into food processor. Add next 6 ingredients. Process until smooth. Transfer to large bowl. Add remaining lentils.

Add cheese and zucchini. Mix well. Shape into balls using 1 tbsp. (15 mL) lentil mixture for each.

(continued on next page)

Arranged Salads

Put cornmeal into shallow dish. Roll balls in cornmeal until well coated. Deep-fry in hot (375°F, 190°C) cooking oil for about 2 minutes until golden. Remove to paper towels to drain.

Arrange salad greens on 8 individual salad plates. Divide and top each with onion and lentil balls.

Parsley Dressing: Process all 8 ingredients in blender until smooth. Makes about 2/3 cup (150 mL) dressing. Drizzle over salad green mixture. Serves 8.

1 serving: 373 Calories; 15.4 g Total Fat (7.3 g Mono, 3.6 g Poly, 3.3 g Sat); 11 mg Cholesterol; 48 g Carbohydrate; 5 g Fibre; 14 g Protein; 524 mg Sodium

Pictured on page 54.

Papaya And Mixed Greens

A very pretty salad with vibrant summer colours and a fresh dressing. This salad is sure to liven up your table!

Mixed salad greens	4 cups	1 L
Medium papaya, seeded (reserve 2 tbsp., 30 mL, seeds) and cut into 1/3 inch (1 cm) cubes	1	1
Medium tomatoes, quartered, seeded and cut into 1/3 inch (1 cm) cubes	2	2
Chopped green onion	1/4 cup	60 mL
MUSTARD DRESSING		
Peanut (or cooking) oil	3 tbsp.	50 mL
White wine vinegar	2 tbsp.	30 mL
Dry mustard	1 tsp.	5 mL
Liquid honey	1 tbsp.	15 mL
Salt	1/4 tsp.	1 mL
Pepper, sprinkle		

Arrange salad greens on 6 individual salad plates.

Top with papaya, tomato and green onion.

Mustard Dressing: Combine all 6 ingredients and reserved papaya seeds in jar with tight-fitting lid. Shake well. Makes 1/2 cup (125 mL) dressing. Drizzle over salad green mixture. Serves 6.

1 serving: 116 Calories; 7.5 g Total Fat (3.3 g Mono, 2.3 g Poly, 1.2 g Sat); 0 mg Cholesterol; 13 g Carbohydrate; 2 g Fibre; 2 g Protein; 120 mg Sodium

Pictured on page 17.

Tomato Basil Salad

A very colourful and attractive salad with a fresh tangy dressing,
topped with crisp goat cheese bread slices for an extra crunch.

Baguette bread slices (about 1/3 inch, 1 cm, thick)	18	18
Olive (or cooking) oil	1 1/2 tbsp.	25 mL
Soft goat (chèvre) cheese	1/2 cup	125 mL
Chopped fresh chives (or 3/4 tsp., 4 mL, dried)	1 tbsp.	15 mL
Chopped fresh mint leaves (or 3/4 tsp., 4 mL, dried)	1 tbsp.	15 mL
Head of butter lettuce, cut or torn	1	1
Cut or torn radicchio	1 cup	250 mL
Halved cherry tomatoes	1 cup	250 mL
Halved yellow cherry tomatoes	1 cup	250 mL
Thinly sliced red onion	1/3 cup	75 mL
TOMATO BASIL DRESSING		
Olive (or cooking) oil	1 1/2 tbsp.	25 mL
Medium tomato, peeled	1	1
Balsamic vinegar	1 tbsp.	15 mL
Chopped fresh sweet basil (or 3/4 tsp., 4 mL, dried)	1 tbsp.	15 mL
Tomato paste (optional)	1 tsp.	5 mL
Granulated sugar	1 tsp.	5 mL
Garlic clove, halved (or 1/4 tsp., 1 mL, powder)	1	1
Salt	1/4 tsp.	1 mL
Pepper, sprinkle		

Brush both sides of each bread slice with olive oil. Bake on ungreased baking sheet in 350°F (175°C) oven for about 10 minutes, turning once, until golden.

Combine cheese, chives and mint in small bowl. Divide and spread on 1 side of each bread slice. Broil 5 inches (12.5 cm) from heat for about 3 minutes until cheese is melted.

Arrange next 5 ingredients on 6 individual salad plates.

(continued on next page)

Tomato Basil Dressing: Process all 9 ingredients in blender until Makes about 3/4 cup (175 mL) dressing. Drizzle over vegetable Top each salad with 3 bread slices. Serves 6.

1 serving: 346 Calories; 16.2 g Total Fat (7 g Mono, 2 g Poly, 5.8 g Sat); 17 mg Cholesterol; 39 g Carbohydrate; 10 g Fibre; 18 g Protein; 440 mg Sodium

Pictured on page 89.

Strawberry Pecan Salad

Crisp spinach is topped with refreshing slices of fresh strawberries in this salad. The addition of candied pecans creates a pleasant texture.

Pecans, toasted (see Tip, page 86)	2/3 cup	150 mL
Granulated sugar	1/2 cup	125 mL
Water	1/4 cup	60 mL
Bag of spinach, stems removed	6 oz.	170 g
Sliced fresh strawberries	2 cups	500 mL
Soft goat (chèvre) cheese, crumbled (optional)	3 oz.	85 g
STRAWBERRY DRESSING		
Olive (or cooking) oil	3 tbsp.	50 mL
Strawberry jam, warmed	2 tbsp.	30 mL
Balsamic vinegar	2 tbsp.	30 mL
Coarsely ground pepper (or 1/8 tsp., 0.5 mL, pepper)	1/4 tsp.	1 mL

Arrange pecans, just touching, in single layer on lightly greased baking sheet.

Combine sugar and water in small saucepan. Heat and stir on low until sugar is dissolved. Boil on medium-high for 5 to 10 minutes, without stirring, until golden brown. Drizzle over pecans. Let stand for about 20 minutes until cool and hard. Chop.

Arrange spinach on 6 individual salad plates. Top with pecan mixture, strawberries and cheese.

Strawberry Dressing: Combine all 4 ingredients in jar with tight-fitting lid. Shake well. Makes about 1/2 cup (125 mL) dressing. Drizzle over spinach mixture. Serves 6.

1 serving: 254 Calories; 15.8 g Total Fat (10.4 g Mono, 2.9 g Poly, 1.6 g Sat); 0 mg Cholesterol; 30 g Carbohydrate; 3 g Fibre; 2 g Protein; 26 mg Sodium

Pictured on page 90.

Lined-Up Salad

*A visually impressive salad with a subtle blue cheese flavour
and a complementary dressing.*

Head of romaine lettuce, cut or torn	1	1
Hard-boiled eggs, chopped	6	6
Bacon slices, cooked crisp and coarsely crumbled	12	12
Chopped cooked chicken (or turkey)	2 cups	500 mL
Large avocados, chopped	2	2
Medium tomatoes, chopped	2	2
Crumbled blue cheese (about 5 oz., 140 g)	1 cup	250 mL
Trimmed watercress	2 cups	500 mL
HONEY MUSTARD DRESSING		
Olive (or cooking) oil	1/3 cup	75 mL
Red wine vinegar	3 tbsp.	50 mL
Crumbled blue cheese (about 1 oz., 28 g)	2 1/2 tbsp.	37 mL
Honey mustard	1 tbsp.	15 mL
Worcestershire sauce	1 tsp.	5 mL
Garlic clove, minced (or 1/4 tsp., 1 mL, powder)	1	1
Salt	1/4 tsp.	1 mL
Coarsely ground pepper (or 1/8 tsp., 0.5 mL, pepper)	1/4 tsp.	1 mL

Arrange lettuce on large serving platter.

Place next 7 ingredients in order given in rows over lettuce.

Honey Mustard Dressing: Combine all 8 ingredients in jar with tight-fitting lid. Shake well. Makes 2/3 cup (150 mL) dressing. Serve with, or drizzle over, vegetable mixture. Serves 6.

1 serving: 714 Calories; 52.5 g Total Fat (27.1 g Mono, 6.2 g Poly, 14.8 g Sat); 342 mg Cholesterol; 12 g Carbohydrate; 3 g Fibre; 50 g Protein; 884 mg Sodium

Pictured on page 18.

Pepper Layered Salad

A fresh-looking salad with lovely, coloured layers. The tuna and vegetables are complemented by the taste of sweet pineapple and crunchy nuts.

Can of pineapple chunks, drained	14 oz.	398 mL
Large green peppers, chopped	2	2
Cans of chunk tuna packed in broth (6 oz., 170 g, each), drained and broken up	2	2
Chopped iceberg lettuce	3 cups	750 mL
Large red peppers, chopped	2	2
Block of cream cheese, softened	8 oz.	250 g
Sour cream	1 cup	250 mL
Dry onion soup mix, stir before measuring	2 tbsp.	30 mL
Chopped fresh parsley (or 1 1/2 tsp., 7 mL, flakes)	2 tbsp.	30 mL
Coarsely chopped pistachios	1/2 cup	125 mL

Layer first 5 ingredients in order given in 16 cup (4 L) deep glass bowl.

Combine cream cheese, sour cream and soup mix in medium bowl. Beat until smooth. Spread in even layer over red pepper. Cover with plastic wrap. Chill overnight.

Just before serving, sprinkle with parsley and pistachios. Serves 10 to 12.

1 serving: 244 Calories; 16.9 g Total Fat (6.2 g Mono, 1.4 g Poly, 8.4 g Sat); 49 mg Cholesterol; 13 g Carbohydrate; 2 g Fibre; 12 g Protein; 465 mg Sodium

Paré Pointer

He said he stole his friend's saw for a joke. Since he lived 5 kilometres away, the judge said he carried the joke too far.

Rio Ranchero Layered Salad

This large, beautiful salad can be made up to two days ahead. Your guests will love the delicious Mexican flavours and the crunchy texture.

Cut or torn romaine lettuce	8 cups	2 L
Hard-boiled eggs, sliced	8	8
Halved cherry tomatoes	3 cups	750 mL
Can of black beans, rinsed and drained	19 oz.	540 mL
Green onions, sliced	4	4
Thinly sliced celery	1/2 cup	125 mL
Medium green pepper, diced	1	1
Cans of kernel corn (7 oz., 199 mL, each), drained	2	2
Large avocados, cubed	2	2
Lime (or lemon) juice	1 tbsp.	15 mL
SASSY SALSA DRESSING		
Mayonnaise (not salad dressing)	1 cup	250 mL
Sour cream	1 cup	250 mL
Finely chopped fresh parsley (or 2 tbsp., 30 mL, flakes)	1/2 cup	125 mL
Chunky salsa	2/3 cup	150 mL
Lime juice	1/3 cup	75 mL
Finely grated lime zest	1/2 tsp.	2 mL
Ground cumin	1/2 tsp.	2 mL
Chili powder	1/2 tsp.	2 mL
Granulated sugar	1/2 tsp.	2 mL
Cherry tomatoes	8	8
Grated sharp Cheddar cheese	3/4 cup	175 mL
Grated Monterey Jack With Jalapeño cheese	3/4 cup	175 mL
Bacon slices, cooked crisp and crumbled (optional)	8	8
Sliced ripe olives	2 tbsp.	30 mL
Diced jalapeño pepper	2 tbsp.	30 mL

Put lettuce into 16 cup (4 L) deep glass bowl. Pack down slightly.

(continued on next page)

Layered Salads

Arrange egg slices upright against side of bowl in decorative manner. Arrange remaining egg slices in single layer over lettuce.

Arrange tomatoes upright against side of bowl in decorative manner.

Layer next 5 ingredients in order given over egg slices.

Toss avocado with lime juice in small bowl. Arrange in single layer over corn.

Sassy Salsa Dressing: Combine first 9 ingredients in medium bowl. Spoon over avocado mixture. Carefully spread right to edge of bowl to seal. Cover with plastic wrap. Chill until ready to serve.

Just before serving, top with remaining 6 ingredients. Makes about 18 cups (4.5 L).

1 cup (250 mL): 276 Calories; 21.6 g Total Fat (10.3 g Mono, 4.5 g Poly, 5.5 g Sat); 118 mg Cholesterol; 14 g Carbohydrate; 3 g Fibre; 9 g Protein; 277 mg Sodium

Pictured on page 71.

Water Chestnut And Pea Salad

A pleasant combination of flavours and textures.
The visible layers make an attractive presentation.

Cut or torn romaine lettuce	4 cups	1 L
Can of water chestnuts, drained and coarsely chopped	8 oz.	227 mL
Sliced green onion	1 cup	250 mL
Frozen peas, thawed	3 cups	750 mL
Mayonnaise (not salad dressing)	1 3/4 cups	425 mL
Granulated sugar	1 tbsp.	15 mL
Lemon juice	1 tbsp.	15 mL
Celery salt	1 tsp.	5 mL
Lemon pepper	1 tsp.	5 mL
Hard-boiled eggs, coarsely chopped	4	4
Bacon slices, cooked crisp and crumbled	10	10

Layer first 4 ingredients in order given in 16 cup (4 L) deep glass bowl.

Combine next 5 ingredients in medium bowl. Spread in even layer over peas. Cover with plastic wrap. Chill overnight.

Just before serving, sprinkle with egg and bacon. Serves 8 to 10.

1 serving: 536 Calories; 47.8 g Total Fat (25.7 g Mono, 14.6 g Poly, 6.1 g Sat); 145 mg Cholesterol; 16 g Carbohydrate; 4 g Fibre; 10 g Protein; 632 mg Sodium

Curry Chicken Layered Salad

A hearty combination of ingredients with a nice amount of spice.
The soft chicken and crunchy vegetables go very well together.

Fresh asparagus, trimmed of tough ends and cut into 1 inch (2.5 cm) pieces	1 lb.	454 g
Boiling water		
Ice water		
Chopped cooked chicken	2 cups	500 mL
Thinly sliced English cucumber (with peel)	2 1/2 cups	625 mL
Can of chickpeas (garbanzo beans), rinsed and drained	19 oz.	540 mL
Salad dressing (or mayonnaise)	2 cups	500 mL
Curry powder	1 tbsp.	15 mL
Chopped fresh chives (or 1 1/2 tsp., 7 mL, dried)	2 tbsp.	30 mL

Blanch asparagus in boiling water in large saucepan for about 3 minutes until bright green. Drain.

Plunge into ice water in large bowl. Let stand for 10 minutes until cold. Drain. Put into 16 cup (4 L) deep glass bowl.

Layer chicken, cucumber and chickpeas in order given over asparagus.

Combine salad dressing and curry powder in small bowl. Spread in even layer over chickpeas. Cover with plastic wrap. Chill overnight.

Just before serving, sprinkle with chives. Serves 8 to 10.

1 serving: 446 Calories; 34.2 g Total Fat (18 g Mono, 11.2 g Poly, 3.1 g Sat); 50 mg Cholesterol; 20 g Carbohydrate; 2 g Fibre; 15 g Protein; 494 mg Sodium

Sweet Curry Chicken Salad

A light green salad with a noticeably sweet curry dressing.
Use some darker lettuce, such as romaine, or fresh spinach for more colour.

Boneless, skinless chicken breast halves (about 4)	1 lb.	454 g
Cooking oil	1 tbsp.	15 mL
Cut or torn iceberg lettuce (or mixed salad greens)	4 cups	1 L
Thinly sliced celery	1/2 cup	125 mL
Slivered red pepper	1/2 cup	125 mL
Green onions, sliced	4	4
SWEET CURRY DRESSING		
Salad dressing (or mayonnaise)	2/3 cup	150 mL
Milk	2 tbsp.	30 mL
Granulated sugar	2 tbsp.	30 mL
Curry powder	2 tsp.	10 mL
Worcestershire sauce	1 tsp.	5 mL
Slivered almonds, toasted (see Tip, page 86), optional	1/3 cup	75 mL

Cook chicken in cooking oil in large frying pan until golden and no longer pink inside. Cut into very thin slices. Set aside.

Combine next 4 ingredients in large bowl.

Sweet Curry Dressing: Combine first 5 ingredients in small bowl. Let stand for 2 to 3 minutes until sugar is dissolved. Stir. Makes 3/4 cup (175 mL) dressing. Drizzle over lettuce mixture. Add chicken. Toss well.

Just before serving, sprinkle with almonds. Makes 8 cups (2 L). Serves 4.

1 serving: 412 Calories; 26.1 g Total Fat (13.8 g Mono, 8.3 g Poly, 2.3 g Sat); 77 mg Cholesterol; 17 g Carbohydrate; 2 g Fibre; 27 g Protein; 307 mg Sodium

Pictured on page 35.

Chef's Salad

A traditional salad which offers a flavourful dressing
to coat a nice variety of vegetables, eggs and meats.

Head of iceberg lettuce, cut or torn	1	1
Slivered medium Cheddar cheese	1 cup	250 mL
Slivered deli chicken slices	1 cup	250 mL
Slivered deli ham slices	1 cup	250 mL
Sliced celery	1 cup	250 mL
Green onions, sliced	6	6
Cherry tomatoes, halved	12	12
Cooked peas	1/2 cup	125 mL
Grated carrot	1/4 cup	60 mL
Hard-boiled eggs, cut into 4 wedges each	6	6
DRESSING		
Mayonnaise (not salad dressing)	1 cup	250 mL
White vinegar	2 tbsp.	30 mL
Granulated sugar	1 tbsp.	15 mL
Paprika	1 tsp.	5 mL
Salt	1 tsp.	5 mL
Pepper	1/4 tsp.	1 mL

Arrange lettuce on large serving platter.

Scatter next 8 ingredients over lettuce.

Arrange egg wedges around edge of serving platter.

Dressing: Combine all 6 ingredients in small bowl. Let stand for 2 to 3 minutes until sugar is dissolved. Stir. Makes 1 1/3 cups (325 mL) dressing. Drizzle over vegetable mixture. Serves 6.

1 serving: 585 Calories; 48 g Total Fat (23.1 g Mono, 12.2 g Poly, 10.2 g Sat); 296 mg Cholesterol; 12 g Carbohydrate; 2 g Fibre; 26 g Protein; 1168 mg Sodium

Variation: Make individual salads by scattering 1/6 of each ingredient over about 2 cups (500 mL) lettuce on individual salad plates. Makes 6.

Broccoli Beef Salad

Chunks of broccoli and red pepper add colour to this creamy dish.

Broccoli florets	3 cups	750 mL
Boiling water		
Ice water		
Rib-eye steaks (about 2)	1 lb.	454 g
Salt	1/4 tsp.	1 mL
Pepper	1/4 tsp.	1 mL
Cooked brown rice (1/2 cup, 125 mL, uncooked)	1 1/2 cups	375 mL
Finely chopped red pepper	2/3 cup	150 mL
Pine nuts, toasted (see Tip, page 86)	1/2 cup	125 mL
CREAMY ORANGE DRESSING		
Sour cream	1/3 cup	75 mL
Plain yogurt	1/4 cup	60 mL
Orange juice	3 tbsp.	50 mL
White wine vinegar	2 tbsp.	30 mL
Grainy mustard	2 tbsp.	30 mL
Liquid honey	1 tbsp.	15 mL
Garlic clove, minced (or 1/4 tsp., 1 mL, powder)	1	1
Salt	1/2 tsp.	2 mL
Finely grated orange zest	1/4 tsp.	1 mL

Blanch broccoli in boiling water in medium saucepan for 3 to 5 minutes until bright green. Drain.

Plunge into ice water in large bowl. Let stand for 10 minutes until cold. Drain. Put into salad bowl.

Sprinkle both sides of each steak with salt and pepper. Preheat electric grill for 5 minutes or gas barbecue to medium-high. Cook steaks on greased grill for about 4 minutes per side until desired doneness. Let stand for 15 minutes. Cut into 1/4 inch (6 mm) thick slices.

Add beef, rice, red pepper and pine nuts to broccoli. Toss gently.

Creamy Orange Dressing: Combine all 9 ingredients in small bowl. Makes about 1 cup (250 mL) dressing. Drizzle over broccoli mixture. Toss gently. Makes about 6 cups (1.5 L). Serves 4.

1 serving: 739 Calories; 30.1 g Total Fat (11.5 g Mono, 6.4 g Poly, 9.5 g Sat); 80 mg Cholesterol; 76 g Carbohydrate; 9 g Fibre; 46 g Protein; 671 mg Sodium

Taco Bean Salad

This healthy meal salad is very easy to prepare. Your family will love the crunch of the corn chips and the spicy kick of the dressing.

Cut or torn romaine lettuce	4 cups	1 L
Can of red kidney beans, rinsed and drained	19 oz.	540 mL
Finely chopped red onion	1/2 cup	125 mL
Corn chips	2 cups	500 mL
JALAPEÑO DRESSING		
Sour cream	1/4 cup	60 mL
Catalina dressing	1/4 cup	60 mL
Coarsely chopped fresh cilantro (or fresh parsley)	2 tbsp.	30 mL
Sliced pickled jalapeño pepper	1 tbsp.	15 mL
Ground cumin	1/4 – 1/2 tsp.	1 – 2 mL
Garlic clove (or 1/4 tsp., 1 mL, powder)	1	1
Medium avocados, chopped	2	2

Put first 4 ingredients into large bowl. Toss.

Jalapeño Dressing: Process first 6 ingredients in blender until smooth. Makes 1/2 cup (125 mL) dressing. Drizzle over lettuce mixture.

Top with avocado. Toss gently. Serve immediately. Makes about 8 cups (2 L). Serves 4.

1 serving: 367 Calories; 25.5 g Total Fat (14.2 g Mono, 4.9 g Poly, 4.4 g Sat); 16 mg Cholesterol; 30 g Carbohydrate; 8 g Fibre; 10 g Protein; 481 mg Sodium

1. Sweet Curry Chicken Salad, page 31
2. Pork And Hazelnut Salad, page 42
3. Shrimp And Asparagus Salad, page 38

Props Courtesy Of: Browne & Co. Ltd.
Wiltshire®

Creamy Chicken Salad

The colourful, creamy dressing coats this salad generously. The blue cheese flavour is mellowed by the sweetness of the raisins.

Spinach, stems removed, lightly packed	6 cups	1.5 L
Coarsely shredded cooked chicken	2 1/2 cups	625 mL
Large red pepper, finely chopped	1	1
Dark raisins	1 cup	250 mL
Slivered almonds, toasted (see Tip, page 86)	2/3 cup	150 mL
Thinly sliced red onion	1/2 cup	125 mL
CREAMY BLUE CHEESE DRESSING		
Mayonnaise (not salad dressing)	1/4 cup	60 mL
Buttermilk (or reconstituted from powder)	1/4 cup	60 mL
Apple cider vinegar	2 tbsp.	30 mL
Crumbled blue cheese (about 1 oz., 28 g)	3 tbsp.	50 mL
Garlic clove, minced (or 1/4 tsp., 1 mL, powder)	1	1

Put first 6 ingredients into large bowl. Toss.

Creamy Blue Cheese Dressing: Process all 5 ingredients in blender until smooth. Makes 1 cup (250 mL) dressing. Drizzle over spinach mixture. Toss. Makes 8 cups (2 L). Serves 4.

1 serving: 605 Calories; 33.3 g Total Fat (17.4 g Mono, 8.3 g Poly, 5.6 g Sat); 97 mg Cholesterol; 44 g Carbohydrate; 6 g Fibre; 38 g Protein; 342 mg Sodium

1. Crab And Pea Salad, page 43
2. Wasabi Pea Salad, page 82
3. Asian Peanut Crunch, page 64

Props Courtesy Of: Island Pottery Inc.
Pier 1 Imports

Shrimp And Asparagus Salad

An attractive salad with specks of mustard seed scattered throughout.
The fresh-tasting dressing is simply delightful! Serve on a bed of butter lettuce.

Fresh asparagus, trimmed of tough ends and cut into 1 inch (2.5 cm) pieces	1 lb.	454 g
Boiling water		
Salt	1/2 tsp.	2 mL
Ice water		
Cooked medium shrimp (about 33), peeled and deveined	1 lb.	454 g
Can of artichoke hearts, drained and quartered	14 oz.	398 mL
Medium tomatoes, diced into 3/4 inch (2 cm) pieces	2	2

GREEN ONION DRESSING

Olive (or cooking) oil	2 tbsp.	30 mL
Chopped green onion	2/3 cup	150 mL
White wine vinegar	1/4 cup	60 mL
Brown sugar, packed	1 tbsp.	15 mL
Olive (or cooking) oil	1/4 cup	60 mL
Grainy mustard	1 tbsp.	15 mL
Salt	1/4 tsp.	1 mL

Cook asparagus in boiling water and salt in large saucepan for 2 to 3 minutes until bright green. Drain.

Plunge into ice water in medium bowl. Let stand for 10 minutes until cold. Drain. Put into salad bowl.

Add shrimp, artichoke hearts and tomato. Toss.

Green Onion Dressing: Heat first amount of olive oil in medium frying pan on medium-low. Add green onion. Cook for about 5 minutes until soft.

Add vinegar and brown sugar. Heat and stir until brown sugar is dissolved. Cool slightly.

(continued on next page)

Process green onion mixture and next 3 ingredients in blender until smooth. Makes about 2/3 cup (150 mL) dressing. Drizzle over asparagus mixture. Toss. Makes about 8 cups (2 L). Serves 4.

1 serving: 387 Calories; 23.2 g Total Fat (16 g Mono, 2.7 g Poly, 3.3 g Sat); 221 mg Cholesterol; 19 g Carbohydrate; 5 g Fibre; 29 g Protein; 643 mg Sodium

Pictured on page 35.

Crunchy Turkey Salad

This elegant salad has a gentle heat in the creamy dressing.
Serve with whole wheat bread or in a pita for something different.

Chopped cooked turkey	2 cups	500 mL
Chopped green pepper	1 cup	250 mL
Chopped celery	1 cup	250 mL
Pistachios (or pecans), toasted (see Tip, page 86) and coarsely chopped	2/3 cup	150 mL
Chopped green onion	1/2 cup	125 mL
Sunflower seeds, toasted (see Tip, page 86)	1/2 cup	125 mL
Chopped fresh sweet basil (or 1 1/2 tsp., 7 mL, dried)	2 tbsp.	30 mL
CREAMY DRESSING		
Mayonnaise (not salad dressing)	1/3 cup	75 mL
Sour cream	1/4 cup	60 mL
Lemon juice	1 tbsp.	15 mL
Sweet (or regular) chili sauce	1 tbsp.	15 mL
Hot pepper sauce	1/2 – 1 tsp.	2 – 5 mL
Pepper	1/4 tsp.	1 mL
Head of butter lettuce, leaves separated	1	1

Put first 7 ingredients into large bowl. Toss.

Creamy Dressing: Combine first 6 ingredients in small bowl. Makes 2/3 cup (150 mL) dressing. Drizzle over turkey mixture. Toss well.

Arrange lettuce on large serving platter. Spoon turkey mixture on top to within 2 inches (5 cm) of edge. Makes about 6 cups (1.5 L). Serves 4 to 6.

1 serving: 556 Calories; 41.9 g Total Fat (19.7 g Mono, 14.4 g Poly, 6.1 g Sat); 91 mg Cholesterol; 18 g Carbohydrate; 3 g Fibre; 31 g Protein; 266 mg Sodium

Spinach Pasta Salad

An inviting salad with a hearty helping of ingredients.
This Greek and Italian blend will leave your guests wanting more.

Lemon juice	2 tbsp.	30 mL
Olive (or cooking) oil	1 tbsp.	15 mL
Garlic clove, minced (or 1/4 tsp., 1 mL, powder)	1	1
Boneless, skinless chicken breast halves (about 2)	1/2 lb.	225 g
Medium bow pasta	2 cups	500 mL
Boiling water	8 cups	2 L
Salt	1/2 tsp.	2 mL
Spinach, stems removed, lightly packed	4 cups	1 L
Chopped tomato	1 cup	250 mL
Coarsely crumbled feta cheese (about 2 1/2 oz., 70 g)	1/2 cup	125 mL
Whole kalamata olives	1/3 cup	75 mL
PARSLEY PESTO DRESSING		
Coarsely chopped fresh parsley (or 2 tbsp., 30 mL, flakes)	1/2 cup	125 mL
Finely grated fresh Parmesan cheese	1/3 cup	75 mL
Olive (or cooking) oil	1/3 cup	75 mL
Pine nuts, toasted (see Tip, page 86)	1/4 cup	60 mL
Red wine vinegar	1/4 cup	60 mL
Garlic cloves, minced (or 1/2 tsp., 2 mL, powder)	2	2
Salt	1/4 tsp.	1 mL
Pepper	1/8 tsp.	0.5 mL

Combine lemon juice, olive oil and garlic in medium bowl. Add chicken. Turn until coated. Preheat electric grill for 5 minutes or gas barbecue to medium. Cook chicken on greased grill for about 5 minutes per side until no longer pink inside. Let stand for 10 minutes. Cut into 1/8 inch (3 mm) thick slices. Keep warm.

Cook pasta in boiling water and salt in large uncovered pot or Dutch oven for 8 to 10 minutes until tender but firm. Drain. Rinse under cold water. Drain well. Transfer to large bowl.

Add chicken and next 4 ingredients. Toss gently.

(continued on next page)

Parsley Pesto Dressing: Process all 8 ingredients in blender until smooth. Makes about 2/3 cup (150 mL) dressing. Drizzle over pasta mixture. Toss gently. Makes about 9 cups (2.25 L). Serves 6.

1 serving: 421 Calories; 25.5 g Total Fat (14.5 g Mono, 3.4 g Poly, 6.2 g Sat); 47 mg Cholesterol; 29 g Carbohydrate; 3 g Fibre; 22 g Protein; 468 mg Sodium

Pictured on page 143.

Coconut Pork Salad

Enjoy the taste of the tropics with this sweet salad. Tender chunks of pork are tossed with coconut and juicy chunks of pineapple. Yum!

Fresh snow pea pods, trimmed	2 cups	500 mL
Fresh sugar snap pea pods, trimmed	1 1/2 cups	375 mL
Boiling water		
Ice water		
Chopped cooked pork	2 cups	500 mL
Pea sprouts	1 cup	250 mL
Unsweetened flake coconut, toasted (see Tip, page 86)	1/2 cup	125 mL
Slivered almonds, toasted (see Tip, page 86)	1/2 cup	125 mL
Can of pineapple chunks, drained	14 oz.	398 mL
CHILI DRESSING		
Sweet (or regular) chili sauce	1/4 cup	60 mL
Peanut (or cooking) oil	3 tbsp.	50 mL
Lime juice	2 tbsp.	30 mL
Fish sauce	2 tsp.	10 mL
Sesame oil	1 tsp.	5 mL

Blanch snow pea pods and sugar snap pea pods in boiling water in large saucepan for about 3 minutes until bright green. Drain.

Plunge into ice water in large bowl. Let stand for 10 minutes until cold. Drain. Put into salad bowl.

Add next 5 ingredients. Toss.

Chili Dressing: Combine all 5 ingredients in jar with tight-fitting lid. Shake well. Makes about 1/2 cup (125 mL) dressing. Drizzle over pork mixture. Toss. Makes about 8 cups (2 L). Serves 4.

1 serving: 598 Calories; 36.7 g Total Fat (14.9 g Mono, 5.9 g Poly, 13.3 g Sat); 64 mg Cholesterol; 40 g Carbohydrate; 7 g Fibre; 33 g Protein; 482 mg Sodium

Pork And Hazelnut Salad

A large hearty salad with a wonderful variety of colours,
flavours and textures. The perfect salad to serve a crowd.

Orange juice	1/2 cup	125 mL
Liquid honey	2 tbsp.	30 mL
Grainy mustard	2 tbsp.	30 mL
Soy sauce	1 tbsp.	15 mL
Finely grated orange zest	1 tsp.	5 mL
Pork tenderloin	1 lb.	454 g
Bag of spinach, stems removed	10 oz.	285 g
Halved cherry tomatoes	2 cups	500 mL
Can of artichoke hearts, drained and quartered	14 oz.	398 mL
Thinly sliced red onion	1 cup	250 mL
Hazelnuts (filberts), toasted (see Tip, page 86) and chopped	1/3 cup	75 mL
Chopped fresh mint leaves (or 3/4 – 2 1/4 tsp., 4 – 11 mL, dried)	1 – 3 tbsp.	15 – 50 mL

HAZELNUT DRESSING

Hazelnut oil	3 tbsp.	50 mL
Balsamic vinegar	2 tbsp.	30 mL
Cooking oil	1 1/2 tbsp.	25 mL
Liquid honey	1 tbsp.	15 mL
Grainy mustard	1 tbsp.	15 mL
Garlic clove, minced (or 1/4 tsp., 1 mL, powder)	1	1
Salt	1/4 tsp.	1 mL

Combine first 5 ingredients in medium bowl.

Put pork into shallow dish or resealable freezer bag. Pour marinade over pork. Stir or turn until coated. Cover or seal. Marinate in refrigerator for at least 3 hours, turning several times. Drain and discard marinade. Preheat gas barbecue to medium. Cook pork on greased grill for about 40 minutes, turning often, until tender. Cover. Let stand for 10 minutes. Cut into thin slices. Keep warm.

Put next 6 ingredients into large bowl.

(continued on next page)

Hazelnut Dressing: Combine all 7 ingredients in jar with tight-fitting lid. Shake well. Makes about 2/3 cup (150 mL) dressing. Drizzle over spinach mixture. Add pork. Toss. Makes about 19 cups (4.75 L). Serves 8 to 10.

1 serving: 240 Calories; 14.7 g Total Fat (9.5 g Mono, 2.2 g Poly, 2 g Sat); 34 mg Cholesterol; 14 g Carbohydrate; 3 g Fibre; 15 g Protein; 333 mg Sodium

Pictured on page 35.

Crab And Pea Salad

The flavours of mint and lime in the dressing are absorbed by the thin rice noodles. You can use fresh crab in place of canned if you prefer.

Rice vermicelli	2 oz.	57 g
Boiling water, to cover		
Fresh pea pods, cut julienne	6 oz.	170 g
Pea sprouts	1 cup	250 mL
Thinly sliced radish	1 cup	250 mL
Chopped green onion	1/2 cup	125 mL
Cans of crabmeat (6 oz., 170 g, each), drained, cartilage removed and flaked	2	2
LIME DRESSING		
Peanut (or cooking) oil	3 tbsp.	50 mL
Chopped fresh mint leaves (or 3/4 – 2 1/4 tsp., 4 – 11 mL, dried)	1 – 3 tbsp.	15 – 50 mL
Sweet (or regular) chili sauce	2 tbsp.	30 mL
Lime juice	1 1/2 tbsp.	25 mL
Fish sauce	2 tsp.	10 mL
Soy sauce	1 tsp.	5 mL

Cover vermicelli with boiling water in medium bowl. Let stand for 20 minutes. Drain. Put into large bowl.

Add next 5 ingredients. Toss.

Lime Dressing: Combine all 6 ingredients in jar with tight-fitting lid. Shake well. Makes 2/3 cup (150 mL) dressing. Drizzle over noodle mixture. Toss. Makes about 6 cups (1.5 L). Serves 4.

1 serving: 316 Calories; 11.7 g Total Fat (4.8 g Mono, 3.5 g Poly, 1.9 g Sat); 0 mg Cholesterol; 36 g Carbohydrate; 4 g Fibre; 20 g Protein; 949 mg Sodium

Pictured on page 36.

Peanutty Chicken Salad

*A warm, spicy salad with crisp, crunchy ingredients
and a tangy, caramel-coloured dressing.*

Cooking oil	2 tsp.	10 mL
Boneless, skinless chicken breast halves (about 3), cut into long, thin strips	3/4 lb.	340 g
Coarsely grated carrot	1/4 cup	60 mL
Spicy peanut sauce	1/4 cup	60 mL
Green onions, sliced	2	2
GINGER PEANUT DRESSING		
Spicy peanut sauce	1/3 cup	75 mL
Rice vinegar	3 tbsp.	50 mL
Lime juice	1 tbsp.	15 mL
Soy sauce	1 tbsp.	15 mL
Liquid honey	1 tbsp.	15 mL
Sesame oil (optional)	2 tsp.	10 mL
Garlic clove, minced (or 1/4 tsp., 1 mL, powder)	1	1
Piece of gingerroot (1/2 inch, 12 mm, thick slice), peeled	1	1
Mixed salad greens	6 cups	1.5 L
Finely shredded cabbage	2 cups	500 mL
Fresh bean sprouts	2 cups	500 mL
Chopped roasted peanuts	2 tbsp.	30 mL

Heat cooking oil in wok or large frying pan on medium-high. Add chicken. Stir-fry for about 2 minutes until beginning to brown.

Add carrot, peanut sauce and green onion. Stir-fry for 2 to 3 minutes until chicken is tender and no longer pink. Remove from heat. Keep warm.

Ginger Peanut Dressing: Process first 8 ingredients in blender until smooth. Makes about 1 cup (250 mL) dressing.

Put salad greens, cabbage and bean sprouts into large bowl. Drizzle with dressing. Toss. Makes about 8 cups (2 L). Arrange on 4 individual salad plates. Divide and arrange chicken mixture on top of each salad.

Sprinkle with peanuts. Serves 4.

1 serving: 345 Calories; 18 g Total Fat (7.5 g Mono, 4.6 g Poly, 4.6 g Sat); 49 mg Cholesterol; 21 g Carbohydrate; 4 g Fibre; 30 g Protein; 931 mg Sodium

Summer Crunch Salad

A bright, beautiful salad with a fresh mix of ingredients and just the right amount of dressing. The spiced croutons add a nice crunch to the soft greens.

CROUTONS		
Hard margarine (or butter), melted	3 tbsp.	50 mL
Garlic salt	1/4 – 1/2 tsp.	1 – 2 mL
Chili powder	1/4 – 1/2 tsp.	1 – 2 mL
Celery salt	1/4 tsp.	1 mL
Unsliced white bread loaf, crust removed, cut into 1/2 inch (12 mm) cubes	1/4	1/4
Mixed salad greens	6 cups	1.5 L
Jar of roasted red peppers, drained and coarsely chopped	13 oz.	370 mL
Large avocado, coarsely chopped	1	1
Thinly sliced red onion	1/2 cup	125 mL
Small pitted ripe whole olives	1/3 cup	75 mL
RED CURRANT DRESSING		
Olive (or cooking) oil	1/4 – 1/3 cup	60 – 75 mL
White wine vinegar	3 tbsp.	50 mL
Red currant jelly	2 – 3 tbsp.	30 – 50 mL
Grainy mustard	1 tbsp.	15 mL
Salt	1/4 tsp.	1 mL
Pepper, just a pinch		

Croutons: Combine first 4 ingredients in large bowl. Add bread. Toss until coated. Arrange in single layer on lightly greased baking sheet. Bake in 375°F (190°C) oven for about 15 minutes, stirring once, until golden and crisp. Cool.

Put next 5 ingredients into separate large bowl. Toss gently.

Red Currant Dressing: Process all 6 ingredients in blender until smooth. Makes 3/4 cup (175 mL) dressing. Drizzle over salad green mixture. Add croutons. Toss gently. Makes about 9 cups (2.25 L).

1 cup (250 mL): 204 Calories; 15.8 g Total Fat (10.4 g Mono, 1.7 g Poly, 2.5 g Sat); trace Cholesterol; 15 g Carbohydrate; 2 g Fibre; 3 g Protein; 376 mg Sodium

Pictured on front cover.

BLT Salad

Who would have thought you could enjoy the great taste of a BLT sandwich in a salad? Tossed with a creamy dressing, this salad will keep you coming back for more!

Bacon slices, diced	8	8
Bread cubes (about 1/2 inch, 12 mm, each)	2 cups	500 mL
Head of green leaf lettuce, cut or torn	1	1
Roma (plum) tomatoes, quartered lengthwise	4	4
BASIL MAYONNAISE DRESSING		
Mayonnaise (not salad dressing)	1/3 cup	75 mL
Finely chopped fresh sweet basil (or 2 1/4 tsp., 11 mL, dried)	3 tbsp.	50 mL
Red wine vinegar	2 tbsp.	30 mL
Salt	1/4 tsp.	1 mL
Coarsely ground pepper (or 1/8 tsp., 0.5 mL, pepper)	1/4 tsp.	1 mL

Cook bacon in large frying pan on medium for 5 to 10 minutes until almost crisp. Remove to paper towels to drain. Reserve 2 tbsp. (30 mL) drippings.

Heat reserved drippings in same frying pan on medium. Add bread. Stir until coated. Heat for 5 to 8 minutes, stirring occasionally, until golden. Remove to paper towels to drain.

Put bacon, lettuce and tomato into large bowl. Toss.

Basil Mayonnaise Dressing: Combine all 5 ingredients in small bowl. Makes about 1/2 cup (125 mL) dressing. Drizzle over lettuce mixture. Toss. Scatter with bread. Makes about 8 cups (2 L).

1 cup (250 mL): 156 Calories; 11.6 g Total Fat (6 g Mono, 3.2 g Poly, 2 g Sat); 11 mg Cholesterol; 10 g Carbohydrate; 2 g Fibre; 4 g Protein; 286 mg Sodium

Endive And Radicchio Salad

The radicchio adds a lot of vibrant colour to this salad. Raisins and dried crushed chilies create a tantalizing mix of sweet and spicy flavours.

Heads of Belgian endive, leaves separated	3	3
Cut or torn radicchio	3 cups	750 mL
Finely chopped green pepper	1 cup	250 mL
Dark raisins	1 cup	250 mL
CILANTRO DRESSING		
Olive (or cooking) oil	3 tbsp.	50 mL
Lemon juice	1 tbsp.	15 mL
Balsamic vinegar	1 tbsp.	15 mL
Chopped fresh cilantro (or fresh parsley)	1 tbsp.	15 mL
Dried crushed chilies	1 tsp.	5 mL
Garlic clove, minced (or 1/4 tsp., 1 mL, powder)	1	1
Salt	1/4 tsp.	1 mL

Put first 4 ingredients into large bowl. Toss.

Cilantro Dressing: Combine all 7 ingredients in jar with tight-fitting lid. Shake well. Makes about 1/3 cup (75 mL) dressing. Drizzle over endive mixture. Toss. Makes about 9 cups (2.25 L).

1 cup (250 mL): 105 Calories; 4.8 g Total Fat (3.4 g Mono, 0.4 g Poly, 0.7 g Sat); 0 mg Cholesterol; 16 g Carbohydrate; 1 g Fibre; 1 g Protein; 75 mg Sodium

Pictured on page 53.

tip *Make sure to keep endive dry. Each head should be wrapped in paper towel and placed inside a plastic bag. Store in refrigerator for up to 24 hours. Wash just before using endive. To prepare Belgian endive, slice and discard 1/8 inch (3 mm) off stem end. Insert a paring knife 1/2 inch (12 mm) into stem end and carve out a cone shape.*

Spinach Squash Salad

An aromatic salad with warm, autumn colours and a delicate nutty undertone.

Sliced peeled butternut squash, cut into 1/8 inch (3 mm) thick slices (about 1/3 medium squash)	1 1/2 cups	375 mL
Fresh medium white mushrooms, halved	12	12
Bag of spinach, stems removed	10 oz.	285 g
Thin prosciutto (or deli) ham slices, cooked crisp and broken into 3/4 inch (2 cm) pieces	6	6
Shaved fresh Parmesan cheese	1/2 cup	125 mL
APPLE SPICE DRESSING		
Olive (or cooking) oil	1/4 cup	60 mL
Apple cider vinegar	2 tbsp.	30 mL
Garlic clove, minced (or 1/4 tsp., 1 mL, powder)	1	1
Ground nutmeg	1/8 tsp.	0.5 mL
Ground cinnamon	1/8 tsp.	0.5 mL
Salt	1/8 tsp.	0.5 mL
Pepper	1/8 tsp.	0.5 mL

Spray both sides of each slice of squash with cooking spray. Preheat electric grill for 5 minutes or gas barbecue to medium. Cook squash on well-greased grill for about 5 minutes per side until tender and browned. Cut into 3/4 inch (2 cm) pieces. Put into large bowl.

Spray mushrooms with cooking spray. Cook on greased grill for about 5 minutes, turning once, until browned. Cut each piece in half. Add to squash.

Add spinach and prosciutto. Toss. Scatter cheese over top.

Apple Spice Dressing: Combine all 7 ingredients in jar with tight-fitting lid. Shake well. Makes 1/3 cup (75 mL) dressing. Drizzle over spinach mixture. Toss. Makes about 6 cups (1.5 L).

1 cup (250 mL): 199 Calories; 15.7 g Total Fat (9.4 g Mono, 1.4 g Poly, 4.1 g Sat); 12 mg Cholesterol; 9 g Carbohydrate; 2 g Fibre; 8 g Protein; 357 mg Sodium

Pictured on page 125 and on back cover.

Mixed Green Salad

A simple salad with toasted macadamia nuts and the refreshing addition of kiwifruit. This would go so well with barbecued or roasted chicken.

Mixed salad greens	6 cups	1.5 L
Thinly sliced red onion	3/4 cup	175 mL
Macadamia nuts, toasted (see Tip, page 86) and coarsely chopped	1/2 cup	125 mL
MUSTARD DRESSING		
Peanut (or cooking) oil	3 tbsp.	50 mL
Red wine vinegar	2 tbsp.	30 mL
Dijon mustard	1 tbsp.	15 mL
Chopped fresh thyme leaves (or 1/4 tsp., 1 mL, dried)	1 tsp.	5 mL
Garlic clove, minced (or 1/4 tsp., 1 mL, powder)	1	1
Salt	1/4 tsp.	1 mL
Kiwifruit, halved lengthwise and sliced	2	2

Put salad greens, onion and macadamia nuts into large bowl. Toss.

Mustard Dressing: Combine first 6 ingredients in jar with tight-fitting lid. Shake well. Makes about 1/2 cup (125 mL) dressing. Drizzle over salad green mixture. Toss.

Add kiwifruit. Toss gently. Makes about 6 cups (1.5 L).

1 cup (250 mL): 188 Calories; 16.2 g Total Fat (10.1 g Mono, 2.5 g Poly, 2.5 g Sat); 0 mg Cholesterol; 11 g Carbohydrate; 3 g Fibre; 3 g Protein; 159 mg Sodium

Paré Pointer

The sure way to win a race is to run faster than anyone else.

Pineapple And Cashew Salad

Taste the tropics in this sweet, crunchy salad. Crisp lettuce leaves are tossed with juicy chunks of pineapple and soft, sweet flakes of coconut. Yum!

Head of romaine lettuce, cut or torn	1	1
Cashews, toasted (see Tip, page 86) and chopped	2/3 cup	150 mL
Can of pineapple chunks, drained and 2 tbsp. (30 mL) juice reserved	14 oz.	398 mL
Thinly sliced red onion	1/2 cup	125 mL
PINEAPPLE DRESSING		
Peanut (or cooking) oil	3 tbsp.	50 mL
Red wine vinegar	2 tbsp.	30 mL
Reserved pineapple juice	2 tbsp.	30 mL
Sweet (or regular) chili sauce	1 tbsp.	15 mL
Salt	1/4 tsp.	1 mL
Coarsely ground pepper (or 1/8 tsp., 0.5 mL, pepper)	1/4 tsp.	1 mL
Flake coconut, toasted (see Tip, page 86)	1/2 cup	125 mL

Put first 4 ingredients into large bowl. Toss.

Pineapple Dressing: Combine first 6 ingredients in jar with tight-fitting lid. Shake well. Makes about 1/2 cup (125 mL) dressing. Drizzle over lettuce mixture.

Add coconut. Toss. Makes about 13 cups (3.25 L).

1 cup (250 mL): 123 Calories; 9.1 g Total Fat (3.6 g Mono, 1.7 g Poly, 3.3 g Sat); 0 mg Cholesterol; 10 g Carbohydrate; 1 g Fibre; 2 g Protein; 69 mg Sodium

---

Paré Pointer
Cheapskates don't last long on the ice.

Spinach Bacon Salad

This satisfying dish is full of fresh, inviting ingredients.
You'll love the smoky bacon aftertaste and the creamy dressing.

CROUTONS

Cooking oil	2 tbsp.	30 mL
Garlic salt	1 tsp.	5 mL
Bread cubes (about 1/2 inch, 12 mm, each)	2 cups	500 mL
Bag of spinach, stems removed (reserve 1/2 cup, 125 mL, packed)	6 oz.	170 g
Hard-boiled eggs, coarsely chopped	3	3
Shaved fresh Parmesan cheese	1/2 cup	125 mL
Bacon slices, cooked crisp and crumbled	6	6

SPINACH DRESSING

Reserved spinach	1/2 cup	125 mL
Bacon slices, cooked crisp and crumbled	2	2
Buttermilk (or reconstituted from powder)	1/3 cup	75 mL
Cooking oil	1/4 cup	60 mL
White wine vinegar	2 tbsp.	30 mL
Chopped fresh parsley (or 1 1/2 tsp., 7 mL, flakes)	2 tbsp.	30 mL
Dijon mustard	1 tbsp.	15 mL
Garlic clove, halved (or 1/4 tsp., 1 mL, powder)	1	1
Granulated sugar	2 tsp.	10 mL
Coarsely ground pepper (or 1/8 tsp., 0.5 mL, pepper)	1/4 tsp.	1 mL

Croutons: Combine cooking oil and garlic salt in medium bowl. Add bread. Toss until coated. Arrange in single layer on lightly greased baking sheet. Bake in 375°F (190°C) oven for about 15 minutes, turning occasionally, until golden and crisp. Cool.

Put next 4 ingredients into large bowl. Toss.

Spinach Dressing: Process all 10 ingredients in food processor until smooth. Makes 1 cup (250 mL) dressing. Drizzle over spinach mixture. Add croutons. Toss. Makes about 8 cups (2 L).

1 cup (250 mL): 233 Calories; 18.5 g Total Fat (9.4 g Mono, 4 g Poly, 3.9 g Sat); 92 mg Cholesterol; 8 g Carbohydrate; 1 g Fibre; 9 g Protein; 503 mg Sodium

Creamy Bibb Lettuce

Serve this salad on chilled plates with this savoury, lemon-flavoured dressing.
Add a fresh fruit garnish to pretty it up for guests.

WHIPPING CREAM DRESSING

Whipping cream	3/4 cup	175 mL
Lemon juice	1 tbsp.	15 mL
Granulated sugar	1 1/2 tsp.	7 mL
Salt	1/2 tsp.	2 mL
Pepper	1/4 tsp.	1 mL
Heads of bibb (or butter) lettuce, cut or torn	2	2
Fresh fruit in season (optional)	1 cup	250 mL

Whipping Cream Dressing: Combine first 5 ingredients in small bowl. Beat until frothy with whisk. Makes about 1 cup (250 mL) dressing.

Put lettuce into large bowl. Drizzle with dressing. Toss gently.

Top individual servings with fruit. Makes 8 cups (2 L).

1 cup (250 mL): 82 Calories; 7.7 g Total Fat (2.2 g Mono, 0.3 g Poly, 4.8 g Sat); 27 mg Cholesterol; 3 g Carbohydrate; 1 g Fibre; 1 g Protein; 159 mg Sodium

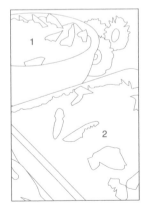

1. Endive And Radicchio Salad, page 47
2. Date And Endive Salad, page 78

Props Courtesy Of: Dansk Gifts

Cucumber Dill Salad

The perfect salad for those who love dill. This crisp, crunchy,
colourful salad is ready to eat in only 15 minutes!

DILL DRESSING		
Plain yogurt	1 cup	250 mL
French dressing	1/4 cup	60 mL
Chopped fresh dill (or 3/4 tsp., 4 mL, dill weed)	1 tbsp.	15 mL
English cucumber (with peel), thinly sliced	1	1
Small red onion, thinly sliced	1	1
Bag of mixed salad greens	12 oz.	340 g

Dill Dressing: Combine yogurt, French dressing and dill in small bowl. Let stand for 10 minutes to blend flavours. Makes 1 1/4 cups (300 mL) dressing.

Put cucumber, onion and salad greens into large bowl. Toss. Drizzle with dressing. Toss gently. Makes 8 cups (2 L).

1 cup (250 mL): 74 Calories; 4.1 g Total Fat (2 g Mono, 1.2 g Poly, 0.6 g Sat); 7 mg Cholesterol; 7 g Carbohydrate; 1 g Fibre; 3 g Protein; 174 mg Sodium

1. Parsley Salad, page 62
2. Cucumber And Couscous Salad, page 101
3. Crispy Lentil Ball Salad, page 22

Props Courtesy Of: La Cache
Pier 1 Imports

Spinach Crouton Salad

A colourful Mediterranean salad with slices
of roasted red pepper and crisp spinach.

Red peppers, quartered	2	2
CROUTONS		
Hard margarine (or butter), melted	2 tbsp.	30 mL
Basil pesto	1 tbsp.	15 mL
Baguette bread slices, cut 1/4 inch (6 mm) thick	14	14
Cut or torn spinach, stems removed, lightly packed	4 cups	1 L
Shaved fresh Parmesan cheese	1/4 cup	60 mL
FETA DRESSING		
Olive (or cooking) oil	3 tbsp.	50 mL
Crumbled feta cheese (about 1 oz., 28 g)	3 tbsp.	50 mL
Balsamic vinegar	1 tbsp.	15 mL
Coarsely chopped fresh thyme leaves (or 1/4 tsp., 1 mL, dried)	1 tsp.	5 mL
Coarsely ground pepper (or 1/8 tsp., 0.5 mL, pepper)	1/4 tsp.	1 mL

Arrange red pepper, skin-side up, on ungreased baking sheet, 6 inches (15 cm) from heat. Broil for 10 to 15 minutes, rearranging as necessary, until skins are blistered and blackened. Remove to medium bowl. Cover with plastic wrap. Let sweat for about 15 minutes until cool enough to handle. Remove and discard skins. Cut into 1/2 inch (12 mm) wide strips. Put into large bowl.

Croutons: Combine margarine and pesto in small bowl. Spread on both sides of each bread slice. Place on lightly greased baking sheet. Bake in 350°F (175°C) oven for about 5 minutes per side until golden and crisp.

Add croutons, spinach and Parmesan cheese to red pepper. Toss.

Feta Dressing: Process all 5 ingredients in blender until smooth. Makes 1/3 cup (75 mL) dressing. Spoon over spinach mixture. Toss. Makes about 5 cups (1.25 L).

1 cup (250 mL): 247 Calories; 18.4 g Total Fat (11.4 g Mono, 1.6 g Poly, 4.4 g Sat);
9 mg Cholesterol; 16 g Carbohydrate; 3 g Fibre; 7 g Protein; 365 mg Sodium

Honey Orange Salad

Pepitas, the inside of pumpkin seeds, add a delicious,
delicate flavour to this sweet and tangy salad.

Large oranges, peeled and separated into segments	2	2
Liquid honey, warmed	1 tbsp.	15 mL
Ground cinnamon	1/4 tsp.	1 mL
Mixed salad greens	4 cups	1 L
Sliced fresh strawberries	1 cup	250 mL
Roasted pepitas	1/2 cup	125 mL
Chopped green onion	1/3 cup	75 mL
TARRAGON DRESSING		
Olive (or cooking) oil	3 tbsp.	50 mL
White wine vinegar	2 tbsp.	30 mL
Liquid honey	1 tbsp.	15 mL
Finely chopped fresh tarragon leaves (or 1/2 tsp., 2 mL, dried)	2 tsp.	10 mL
Dry sherry	1 tsp.	5 mL
Salt	1/4 tsp.	1 mL

Put orange, honey and cinnamon into medium bowl. Toss. Chill for 1 hour to blend flavours. Drain and discard any liquid. Transfer to large bowl.

Add next 4 ingredients. Toss.

Tarragon Dressing: Combine all 6 ingredients in jar with tight-fitting lid. Shake well. Makes about 1/3 cup (75 mL) dressing. Drizzle over salad green mixture. Toss gently. Makes about 6 1/2 cups (1.6 L).

1 cup (250 mL): 217 Calories; 14.5 g Total Fat (7.1 g Mono, 4.2 g Poly, 2.3 g Sat); 0 mg Cholesterol; 18 g Carbohydrate; 5 g Fibre; 8 g Protein; 110 mg Sodium

---

Paré Pointer

She turned the heat up in the living room because
she heard roses grew better in a hot house.

Crunchy Spinach Salad

The caramelized green onion in the dressing gives this salad a wonderful sweet flavour, while the water chestnuts and chow mein noodles add a crunch.

Spinach, stems removed, lightly packed	6 cups	1.5 L
Halved cherry tomatoes	2 cups	500 mL
Can of sliced water chestnuts, drained	8 oz.	227 mL
Bacon slices, cooked crisp and crumbled	8	8
GREEN ONION DRESSING		
Olive (or cooking) oil	3 tbsp.	50 mL
Chopped green onion	1/3 cup	75 mL
Garlic clove, minced (or 1/4 tsp., 1 mL, powder)	1	1
Balsamic vinegar	2 tbsp.	30 mL
Worcestershire sauce	1 tsp.	5 mL
Brown sugar, packed	1 tsp.	5 mL
Dry chow mein noodles	2 cups	500 mL

Put first 4 ingredients into large bowl. Toss.

Green Onion Dressing: Heat olive oil in small frying pan on medium-low. Add green onion and garlic. Cook for about 5 minutes until onion is soft.

Process onion mixture, vinegar, Worcestershire sauce and brown sugar in blender until smooth. Makes about 1/3 cup (75 mL) dressing. Drizzle over spinach mixture.

Add noodles. Toss. Makes about 8 cups (2 L).

1 cup (250 mL): 173 Calories; 9.2 g Total Fat (5.5 g Mono, 1.1 g Poly, 2 g Sat); 19 mg Cholesterol; 18 g Carbohydrate; 3 g Fibre; 6 g Protein; 219 mg Sodium

 tip   *To revitalize limp greens, soak them in cold water with a touch of lemon juice or vinegar.*

Curry Hash Brown Salad

If you're in the mood for something a little different, try this tasty salad. Fresh spinach is tossed with a tangy, creamy dressing and golden, curried hash browns. This salad contains a nice variety of colours, flavours and textures.

Frozen hash brown potatoes	1 1/2 cups	375 mL
Olive (or cooking) oil	2 tbsp.	30 mL
Curry powder	1 tbsp.	15 mL
Garlic salt	1/2 tsp.	2 mL
Spinach, stems removed, lightly packed	4 cups	1 L
Thinly sliced onion	1/2 cup	125 mL
Chopped dried apricot	1/2 cup	125 mL
CREAMY DRESSING		
Buttermilk (or reconstituted from powder)	2 tbsp.	30 mL
Whipping cream (or milk)	2 tbsp.	30 mL
Finely chopped green onion	2 tbsp.	30 mL
Chopped fresh parsley (or 3/4 tsp., 4 mL, flakes)	1 tbsp.	15 mL
Olive (or cooking) oil	1 tbsp.	15 mL
Lemon juice	1 tbsp.	15 mL
Salt, sprinkle		
Pepper, sprinkle		
Large avocado, thinly sliced	1	1

Combine first 4 ingredients in large bowl. Toss until coated. Arrange in single layer on lightly greased baking sheet. Bake in 375°F (190°C) oven for about 25 minutes, turning occasionally, until potatoes are golden and crisp.

Put spinach, onion and apricot into separate large bowl. Toss.

Creamy Dressing: Combine first 8 ingredients in jar with tight-fitting lid. Shake well. Makes 1/2 cup (125 mL) dressing. Drizzle over spinach mixture. Add potatoes. Toss.

Top with avocado. Makes about 6 cups (1.5 L).

1 cup (250 mL): 235 Calories; 15.4 g Total Fat (9.4 g Mono, 1.6 g Poly, 3.1 g Sat); 6 mg Cholesterol; 24 g Carbohydrate; 4 g Fibre; 4 g Protein; 156 mg Sodium

Corn And Tomato Salad

This salad takes a little more time to prepare, but it is worth it! Fresh corn kernels liven up the crisp greens and add a hint of sweetness to the salad.

Corncobs, silk and husks removed	2	2
Boiling water		
Salt	1/2 tsp.	2 mL
Medium green peppers, quartered	2	2
Halved cherry tomatoes	2 cups	500 mL
Thinly sliced red onion	3/4 cup	175 mL
Head of romaine lettuce, cut or torn	1	1
Chopped fresh mint leaves (or 1 tbsp., 15 mL, dried)	1/4 cup	60 mL
SWEET CHILI DRESSING		
Olive (or cooking) oil	1/4 cup	60 mL
Sweet (or regular) chili sauce	3 tbsp.	50 mL
White wine vinegar	2 tbsp.	30 mL
Salt	1/4 tsp.	1 mL
Garlic clove, minced (or 1/4 tsp., 1 mL, powder)	1	1

Cook corncobs in boiling water and salt in large pot or Dutch oven for about 3 minutes until tender-crisp. Drain well. Cool. Slice kernels from cobs in strips about 2 inches (5 cm) long.

Arrange green pepper, skin-side up, on ungreased baking sheet, 6 inches (15 cm) from heat. Broil for 10 to 15 minutes, rearranging as necessary, until skins are blistered and blackened. Remove to medium bowl. Cover with plastic wrap. Let sweat for about 15 minutes until cool enough to handle. Remove and discard skins. Cut into 2 inch (5 cm) long strips.

Put corn, green pepper and next 4 ingredients into large bowl. Toss gently.

Sweet Chili Dressing: Combine all 5 ingredients in jar with tight-fitting lid. Shake well. Makes 2/3 cup (150 mL) dressing. Drizzle over lettuce mixture. Toss gently. Makes about 12 cups (3 L).

1 cup (250 mL): 91 Calories; 5.3 g Total Fat (3.6 g Mono, 0.6 g Poly, 0.7 g Sat); 0 mg Cholesterol; 11 g Carbohydrate; 2 g Fibre; 2 g Protein; 117 mg Sodium

Pictured on page 71.

Fennel Parmesan Salad

*Fresh fennel, Parmesan cheese and fresh sweet basil are
a very tasty combination. The light dressing blends so well
with the flavours of the fresh herbs and vegetables.*

Fennel bulb (white part only), thinly sliced	1	1
Head of butter lettuce, cut or torn	1	1
Coarsely grated fresh Parmesan cheese	1/2 cup	125 mL
Chopped fresh sweet basil (or 1 1/2 tsp., 7 mL, dried)	2 tbsp.	30 mL
Chopped fresh parsley (or 1 1/2 tsp., 7 mL, flakes)	2 tbsp.	30 mL
Thinly sliced red onion	1/2 cup	125 mL
RASPBERRY DRESSING		
Olive (or cooking) oil	3 tbsp.	50 mL
Raspberry vinegar	2 tbsp.	30 mL
Balsamic vinegar	1 tbsp.	15 mL
Garlic clove, minced (or 1/4 tsp., 1 mL, powder)	1	1
Salt	1/4 tsp.	1 mL
Pepper	1/4 tsp.	1 mL

Put first 6 ingredients into large bowl. Toss.

Raspberry Dressing: Combine all 6 ingredients in jar with tight-fitting lid.
Shake well. Makes 1/3 cup (75 mL) dressing. Drizzle over lettuce mixture.
Toss. Makes about 6 cups (1.5 L).

*1 cup (250 mL): 125 Calories; 9.7 g Total Fat (5.8 g Mono, 0.7 g Poly, 2.6 g Sat); 7 mg Cholesterol;
6 g Carbohydrate; 1 g Fibre; 5 g Protein; 286 mg Sodium*

Pictured on page 72.

 *Always dry lettuce leaves thoroughly after washing. If being stored, dry
leaves will last longer in refrigerator. When serving, salad dressing will
coat the dry leaves more easily and evenly.*

Parsley Salad

This is such a great way to use all of that parsley growing in your garden.
The citrus dressing makes this healthy salad fresh and fragrant.

Chopped fresh parsley	3 cups	750 mL
Chopped seeded tomato	2 cups	500 mL
Chopped red onion	1 cup	250 mL
Finely chopped green pepper	1 cup	250 mL
Crumbled feta cheese (about 3 oz., 85 g)	2/3 cup	150 mL
LEMON DRESSING		
Lemon juice	2 tbsp.	30 mL
Olive (or cooking) oil	2 tbsp.	30 mL
Chopped fresh mint leaves (or 1 1/2 tsp., 7 mL, dried)	2 tbsp.	30 mL
Garlic cloves, minced (or 1/2 tsp., 2 mL, powder)	2	2
Finely grated lemon zest	1/4 tsp.	1 mL
Salt	1/4 tsp.	1 mL
Coarsely ground pepper (or 1/8 tsp., 0.5 mL, pepper)	1/4 tsp.	1 mL

Put first 5 ingredients into large bowl. Toss.

Lemon Dressing: Combine all 7 ingredients in jar with tight-fitting lid. Shake well. Makes 1/4 cup (60 mL) dressing. Drizzle over vegetable mixture. Toss. Makes about 6 cups (1.5 L).

1 cup (250 mL): 131 Calories; 9 g Total Fat (4.3 g Mono, 0.7 g Poly, 3.4 g Sat); 16 mg Cholesterol; 10 g Carbohydrate; 1 g Fibre; 5 g Protein; 326 mg Sodium

Pictured on page 54.

Paré Pointer

That dog is pretty dirty. He's even prettier when he's clean.

Tossed Salads

Chunky Vegetable Salad

This savoury dressing has a flavour that is unsurpassed! This large recipe is perfect for a buffet or a summertime barbecue. The list is long but easy to prepare.

FLAVOURFUL DRESSING

Olive (or cooking) oil	1/3 cup	75 mL
Coarsely chopped onion	1/4 cup	60 mL
Coarsely chopped carrot	1/4 cup	60 mL
Garlic cloves (or 1/2 – 3/4 tsp., 2 – 4 mL, powder)	2 – 3	2 – 3
Large egg	1	1
White wine vinegar	2 tbsp.	30 mL
Granulated sugar	1 tbsp.	15 mL
Anchovy paste	2 – 3 tsp.	10 – 15 mL
Capers, drained (optional)	1 tsp.	5 mL
Dried whole oregano	1/2 tsp.	2 mL
Paprika	1/2 tsp.	2 mL
Celery seed	1/4 tsp.	1 mL
Salt	1/4 tsp.	1 mL
Pepper, heavy sprinkle		
English cucumber (with peel), cut into cubes	1	1
Green pepper, cut into 3/4 inch (2 cm) pieces	1	1
Yellow pepper, cut into 3/4 inch (2 cm) pieces	1	1
Medium tomatoes, some seeds removed, cut into cubes	2	2
Chopped iceberg lettuce (about 1 1/2 inch, 3.8 cm, chunks)	6 cups	1.5 L
Crumbled feta cheese (about 3 oz., 85 g), optional	2/3 cup	150 mL

Flavourful Dressing: Process first 14 ingredients in blender for about 2 minutes until smooth. Chill for at least 30 minutes to blend flavours. Makes about 1 cup (250 mL) dressing.

Put cucumber, green and yellow peppers and tomato into large bowl. Drizzle with dressing. Toss.

Add lettuce and cheese. Toss. Makes 12 cups (3 L).

1 cup (250 mL): 91 Calories; 7.1 g Total Fat (4.9 g Mono, 0.7 g Poly, 1 g Sat); 19 mg Cholesterol; 6 g Carbohydrate; 1 g Fibre; 2 g Protein; 104 mg Sodium

Asian Peanut Crunch

A fresh, sweet salad with a nice variety of vegetables coated in a peanut satay dressing. The dates in the dressing provide a pleasant sweetness.

SWEET PEANUT DRESSING

Chopped dates	3 tbsp.	50 mL
Boiling water	1/2 cup	125 mL
Smooth peanut butter	2 tbsp.	30 mL
Peanut (or cooking) oil	1 1/2 tbsp.	25 mL
Brown sugar, packed	2 tsp.	10 mL
Lime (or lemon) juice	2 tsp.	10 mL
Sesame oil (optional)	1/2 tsp.	2 mL
Chili paste (sambal oelek)	3/4 tsp.	4 mL
Salt	3/4 tsp.	4 mL
Garlic clove (or 1/4 tsp., 1 mL, powder)	1	1
Cut or torn iceberg lettuce	2 cups	500 mL
Sliced English cucumber (with peel), cut on sharp diagonal	1 cup	250 mL
Cut or torn spinach, stems removed, lightly packed	1 cup	250 mL
Finely shredded cabbage, packed	1 cup	250 mL
Fresh bean sprouts	1 cup	250 mL
Finely sliced red pepper, cut into 2 inch (5 cm) pieces	1/2 cup	125 mL
Roasted salted peanuts, coarsely chopped	1/4 cup	60 mL

Sweet Peanut Dressing: Soak dates in boiling water in small bowl for 15 minutes. Transfer to blender.

Add next 8 ingredients. Process for about 1 minute until smooth. Let stand at room temperature for 30 minutes to blend flavours. Makes about 3/4 cup (175 mL) dressing.

Put next 6 ingredients into large bowl. Drizzle with dressing. Toss.

Sprinkle with peanuts. Makes 8 cups (2 L).

1 cup (250 mL): 104 Calories; 7 g Total Fat (3.3 g Mono, 2.1 g Poly, 1.2 g Sat); 0 mg Cholesterol; 9 g Carbohydrate; 2 g Fibre; 3 g Protein; 292 mg Sodium

Pictured on page 36.

Exotic Spinach Salad

A nice mix of fresh spinach and fruit coated in a thick, sweet dressing.
Before tossing this salad with dressing, set some fruit aside to use as a garnish.

DRESSING

Cooking oil	1/2 cup	125 mL
Granulated sugar	1/4 cup	60 mL
Sesame seeds	2 tbsp.	30 mL
Sliced green onion	1 tbsp.	15 mL
Paprika	1/2 tsp.	2 mL
Worcestershire sauce	1/4 tsp.	1 mL
Poppy seeds	1 1/2 tsp.	7 mL
Apple cider vinegar	1/4 cup	60 mL
Poppy seeds	1 1/2 tsp.	7 mL
Bag of spinach, stems removed	10 oz.	300 g
Medium kiwifruit, sliced	1	1
Sliced fresh strawberries	1 cup	250 mL
Medium mango (or canned, drained), diced (about 3/4 cup, 175 mL)	1/2	1/2
Medium papaya, seeded and diced (about 3/4 cup, 175 mL)	1/2	1/2

Dressing: Process first 7 ingredients in blender for 5 seconds.

With motor running, slowly add vinegar through hole in lid. Process until thick and smooth. Stir in second amount of poppy seeds. Makes 1 cup (250 mL) dressing.

Put remaining 5 ingredients into large bowl. Drizzle with dressing. Toss. Makes 8 cups (2 L).

1 cup (250 mL): 211 Calories; 16.4 g Total Fat (9 g Mono, 5.2 g Poly, 1.3 g Sat); 0 mg Cholesterol; 17 g Carbohydrate; 3 g Fibre; 2 g Protein; 35 mg Sodium

Roasted Veggie Salad

The vegetable portion of this salad can be prepared a day ahead.
This bright, colourful salad is sure to become a favourite!

Red medium pepper, quartered	1	1
Medium zucchini (with peel), cut into 1/4 inch (6 mm) thick slices	1	1
Thinly sliced yam (or sweet potato)	1 cup	250 mL
BALSAMIC DRESSING		
Olive (or cooking) oil	3 tbsp.	50 mL
Balsamic vinegar	2 tbsp.	30 mL
Honey mustard	1 tbsp.	15 mL
Garlic clove, minced (or 1/4 tsp., 1 mL, powder)	1	1
Chopped fresh thyme leaves (or 1/2 tsp., 2 mL, dried)	1 1/2 tsp.	7 mL
Salt	1/4 tsp.	1 mL
Spinach, stems removed, lightly packed	4 cups	1 L

Preheat electric grill for 5 minutes or gas barbecue to medium. Spray red pepper with cooking spray. Arrange red pepper, skin-side down, on greased grill. Cook for 10 to 15 minutes until skins are blistered and blackened. Remove to medium bowl. Cover with plastic wrap. Let sweat for about 15 minutes until cool enough to handle. Remove and discard skins. Cut into thin slices. Put into large bowl.

Cook zucchini on greased grill for about 5 minutes per side until grill marks appear. Add to red pepper. Cook yam on greased grill for 3 to 5 minutes per side until tender. Add to red pepper mixture.

Balsamic Dressing: Combine first 6 ingredients in jar with tight-fitting lid. Shake well. Makes about 1/2 cup (125 mL) dressing. Drizzle over vegetables. Toss. Cover. Chill for 30 to 60 minutes to blend flavours.

Add spinach. Toss. Makes about 6 cups (1.5 L).

1 cup (250 mL): 121 Calories; 7.2 g Total Fat (5.1 g Mono, 0.8 g Poly, 1 g Sat); 0 mg Cholesterol; 14 g Carbohydrate; 3 g Fibre; 2 g Protein; 154 mg Sodium

Cranberry Brie Salad

A colourful, delicately flavoured salad with soft bites of Brie,
tangy dried cranberries and crunchy croutons. This salad
would be great as an appetizer to any meal.

Dried cranberries	1/2 cup	125 mL
Port wine	1/4 cup	60 mL
Brie cheese, chopped	4 oz.	113 g
Head of butter lettuce, cut or torn	1	1
Seasoned croutons	2/3 cup	150 mL
CRANBERRY DRESSING		
Olive (or cooking) oil	2 tbsp.	30 mL
Cranberry cocktail (or orange juice)	2 tbsp.	30 mL
Basil pesto	1 tbsp.	15 mL
Red wine vinegar	1 tbsp.	15 mL

Measure cranberries and port into small bowl. Let stand for 1 hour, stirring occasionally. Drain. Discard port.

Put cranberries, cheese, lettuce and croutons into large bowl. Toss.

Cranberry Dressing: Combine all 4 ingredients in jar with tight-fitting lid. Shake well. Makes 1/3 cup (75 mL) dressing. Drizzle over lettuce mixture. Toss. Makes 6 cups (1.5 L).

1 cup (250 mL): 188 Calories; 12.9 g Total Fat (6.6 g Mono, 0.8 g Poly, 4.7 g Sat); 21 mg Cholesterol; 11 g Carbohydrate; 2 g Fibre; 5 g Protein; 193 mg Sodium

Pictured on page 107.

 tip *To safely clean raw produce, always wash in warm water. Use a scrub brush to remove any surface dirt if the outer skin is to be consumed. For lettuce and other leafy greens, remove and discard outer leaves and then rinse each leaf individually. Special washes, soaps or detergents are not recommended and not necessary for cleaning fruits or vegetables.*

Toffee Nut And Spinach Salad

A delicious change from the ordinary! This salad is tossed with sweet,
crunchy caramelized almonds and drizzled with a fresh, tangy dressing.

Slivered almonds, toasted (see Tip, page 86)	1/2 cup	125 mL
Granulated sugar	1/2 cup	125 mL
Water	1/4 cup	60 mL
Spinach, stems removed, lightly packed	5 cups	1.25 L
Can of mandarin orange segments, drained and 3 tbsp. (50 mL) juice reserved	10 oz.	284 mL

SOUR CREAM DRESSING

Sour cream	1/4 cup	60 mL
Reserved mandarin orange juice	3 tbsp.	50 mL
White wine vinegar	1 tbsp.	15 mL
Grainy mustard	2 tsp.	10 mL
Salt	1/8 tsp.	0.5 mL

Arrange almonds in single layer, just touching, on lightly greased baking sheet.

Put sugar and water into small saucepan. Heat and stir on low until sugar is dissolved. Boil on medium-high for about 10 minutes, without stirring, until sugar mixture is golden brown. Drizzle over almonds. Let stand for about 20 minutes until cool and hard. Chop coarsely.

Put spinach and orange segments into large bowl. Toss.

Sour Cream Dressing: Combine all 5 ingredients in jar with tight-fitting lid. Shake well. Makes 2/3 cup (150 mL) dressing. Drizzle over spinach mixture. Add almonds. Toss. Makes about 8 cups (2 L).

1 cup (250 mL): 137 Calories; 5.8 g Total Fat (3.2 g Mono, 1.1 g Poly, 1.1 g Sat); 3 mg Cholesterol; 20 g Carbohydrate; 2 g Fibre; 3 g Protein; 94 mg Sodium

Pictured on page 107.

Cantaloupe And Prosciutto Salad

Crispy pesto croutons add crunch and colour to this pale green salad.
The Parmesan and garlic dressing goes well with the crispy prosciutto.
Use honeydew instead of cantaloupe for a different look and a sweeter taste.

CROUTONS

Bread cubes (about 1/3 inch, 1 cm, each)	1 cup	250 mL
Basil pesto	2 tbsp.	30 mL
Peanut (or cooking) oil	1 tbsp.	15 mL
Head of butter lettuce, cut or torn	1	1
Medium cantaloupe, thinly sliced	1/2	1/2
Thin prosciutto (or ham) slices, cooked crisp and crumbled	8	8

PARMESAN DRESSING

Peanut (or cooking) oil	1/4 cup	60 mL
Finely grated fresh Parmesan cheese	3 tbsp.	50 mL
Red wine vinegar	2 tbsp.	30 mL
Garlic clove, minced (or 1/4 tsp., 1 mL, powder)	1	1
Salt	1/4 tsp.	1 mL
Coarsely ground pepper (or 1/8 tsp., 0.5 mL, pepper)	1/4 tsp.	1 mL

Croutons: Combine bread, pesto and peanut oil in medium bowl. Toss until coated. Arrange in single layer on lightly greased baking sheet. Bake in 375°F (190°C) oven for about 10 minutes, turning once, until golden and crisp. Cool.

Put lettuce, cantaloupe and prosciutto into large bowl. Toss.

Parmesan Dressing: Process all 6 ingredients in blender until smooth. Makes 1/2 cup (125 mL) dressing. Drizzle over lettuce mixture. Add croutons. Toss. Makes about 8 cups (2 L).

1 cup (250 mL): 165 Calories; 14.2 g Total Fat (6.7 g Mono, 3.4 g Poly, 3.3 g Sat); 7 mg Cholesterol; 6 g Carbohydrate; 1 g Fibre; 4 g Protein; 249 mg Sodium

Fennel And Hazelnut Salad

The sweet, delicate, anise flavour of fresh fennel goes so well
with the sweet dressing and subtle hazelnut aftertaste.

Mixed salad greens	4 cups	1 L
Fennel bulb (white part only), thinly sliced	1	1
Chopped Asiago cheese	1 cup	250 mL
Hazelnuts (filberts), toasted (see Tip, page 86) and coarsely chopped	2/3 cup	150 mL
Thinly sliced red onion	1/2 cup	125 mL
MAPLE DRESSING		
Olive (or cooking) oil	3 tbsp.	50 mL
Balsamic vinegar	2 tbsp.	30 mL
Maple (or maple-flavoured) syrup	2 tbsp.	30 mL
Dry mustard	1 tsp.	5 mL
Salt	1/4 tsp.	1 mL
Garlic clove, minced (or 1/4 tsp., 1 mL, powder)	1	1

Put first 5 ingredients into large bowl. Toss.

Maple Dressing: Combine all 6 ingredients in jar with tight-fitting lid. Shake well. Makes about 1/2 cup (125 mL) dressing. Drizzle over salad green mixture. Toss. Makes about 7 cups (1.75 L).

1 cup (250 mL): 248 Calories; 20 g Total Fat (12.4 g Mono, 1.6 g Poly, 4.8 g Sat); 20 mg Cholesterol; 11 g Carbohydrate; 2 g Fibre; 9 g Protein; 252 mg Sodium

1. Rio Ranchero Layered Salad, page 28
2. Corn And Tomato Salad, page 59
3. Tortilla Jicama Salad, page 77

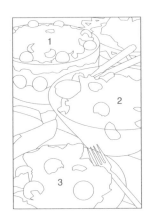

Tomato Mozzarella Salad

This tangy, colourful salad can also double as a pasta sauce.
Heat the salad with dressing in a large saucepan until the
spinach is wilted and the mixture is hot. Toss with hot pasta.

Bag of spinach, stems removed	6 oz.	170 g
Halved cherry tomatoes	1 cup	250 mL
Halved yellow cherry tomatoes	1 cup	250 mL
Chopped mozzarella cheese	1 cup	250 mL
Shredded fresh sweet basil (not dried)	2 tbsp.	30 mL
BALSAMIC DRESSING		
Olive (or cooking) oil	3 tbsp.	50 mL
Balsamic vinegar	2 tbsp.	30 mL
Garlic clove, minced (or 1/4 tsp., 1 mL, powder)	1	1
Salt	1/4 tsp.	1 mL
Pepper	1/4 tsp.	1 mL

Put first 5 ingredients into large bowl. Toss.

Balsamic Dressing: Combine all 5 ingredients in jar with tight-fitting lid. Shake well. Makes about 1/3 cup (75 mL) dressing. Drizzle over spinach mixture. Toss. Makes about 7 cups (1.75 L).

1 cup (250 mL): 126 Calories; 10.6 g Total Fat (5.7 g Mono, 0.7 g Poly, 3.5 g Sat); 16 mg Cholesterol; 4 g Carbohydrate; 1 g Fibre; 5 g Protein; 184 mg Sodium

Pictured on page 72.

1. Creamy Balsamic Romaine Hearts, page 11
2. Tomato Mozzarella Salad, above
3. Fennel Parmesan Salad, page 61

Props Courtesy Of: Casa Bugatti
Pier 1 Imports

Pesto Caesar Salad

This is your classic Caesar salad with a twist! Homemade sun-dried tomato croutons and crispy pieces of prosciutto are tossed in a rich, creamy dressing.

CROUTONS		
Sun-dried tomato pesto	3 tbsp.	50 mL
Olive (or cooking) oil	1 tbsp.	15 mL
Bread cubes (about 1/2 inch, 12 mm, each)	2 cups	500 mL
Head of romaine lettuce, cut or torn	1	1
Thin prosciutto (or deli) ham slices, cooked crisp and crumbled	6	6
Shaved fresh Parmesan cheese	1/3 cup	75 mL
DRESSING		
Olive (or cooking) oil	1/4 cup	60 mL
Finely grated fresh Parmesan cheese	3 tbsp.	50 mL
Lemon juice	2 tbsp.	30 mL
Large egg, soft-boiled	1	1
Anchovy fillet (or 1/2 tsp., 2 mL, anchovy paste)	1	1
Salt	1/8 tsp.	0.5 mL
Coarsely ground pepper (or 1/8 tsp., 0.5 mL, pepper)	1/4 tsp.	1 mL

Croutons: Combine pesto and olive oil in medium bowl. Add bread. Toss until coated. Arrange in single layer on lightly greased baking sheet. Bake in 375°F (190°C) oven for about 15 minutes, turning occasionally, until golden and crisp.

Put lettuce, prosciutto and cheese into large bowl. Toss.

Dressing: Process all 7 ingredients in blender until smooth. Makes about 2/3 cup (150 mL) dressing. Drizzle over lettuce mixture. Add croutons. Toss. Makes about 8 cups (2 L).

1 cup (250 mL): 178 Calories; 14.2 g Total Fat (8.8 g Mono, 1.3 g Poly, 3.3 g Sat); 35 mg Cholesterol; 7 g Carbohydrate; 1 g Fibre; 6 g Protein; 290 mg Sodium

Fruity Butter Lettuce Salad

An inviting summer salad with a light, sweet and sour taste.
The sliced almonds add a nice crunch and a subtle flavour to this dish.

Head of butter lettuce, cut or torn	1	1
Medium oranges, peeled and separated into segments	2	2
Sliced fresh strawberries	2/3 cup	150 mL
Feta cheese, crumbled (about 2 1/2 oz., 70 g)	1/2 cup	125 mL
Sliced almonds, toasted (see Tip, page 86)	1/2 cup	125 mL
ORANGE DRESSING		
Olive (or cooking) oil	2 tbsp.	30 mL
Orange juice	2 tbsp.	30 mL
White wine vinegar	1 tbsp.	15 mL
Granulated sugar	2 tsp.	10 mL
Salt	1/4 tsp.	1 mL
Sesame oil	1/4 tsp.	1 mL
Pepper, just a pinch		

Put first 5 ingredients into large bowl. Toss gently.

Orange Dressing: Combine all 7 ingredients in jar with tight-fitting lid. Shake well. Makes about 1/3 cup (75 mL) dressing. Drizzle over lettuce mixture. Toss gently. Makes about 8 cups (2 L).

1 cup (250 mL): 114 Calories; 8.9 g Total Fat (5.3 g Mono, 1.2 g Poly, 1.9 g Sat); 7 mg Cholesterol; 7 g Carbohydrate; 2 g Fibre; 3 g Protein; 159 mg Sodium

Pictured on page 125 and on back cover.

Paré Pointer

The main difference between lightning and electricity
is that we have to pay for electricity.

Cabbage And Wasabi Pea Salad

A pretty, pale salad with chunks of peaches and a sweet dressing.
Use fresh peaches when they are in season for a special treat.
The wasabi peas add loads of flavour and texture to this salad.

Shredded suey choy (Chinese cabbage)	8 cups	2 L
Chopped green onion	1/2 cup	125 mL
Chopped celery	1/2 cup	125 mL
GOLDEN SYRUP DRESSING		
Peanut (or olive) oil	1/4 cup	60 mL
Apple cider vinegar	2 tbsp.	30 mL
Golden corn syrup	2 tbsp.	30 mL
Finely grated peeled gingerroot	1/2 tsp.	2 mL
Salt	1/4 tsp.	1 mL
Wasabi peas (hot green peas), see Note	1 cup	250 mL
Can of sliced peaches, drained and coarsely chopped	14 oz.	398 mL

Put suey choy, green onion and celery into large bowl. Toss.

Golden Syrup Dressing: Combine first 5 ingredients in jar with tight-fitting lid. Shake well. Makes about 1/2 cup (125 mL) dressing. Drizzle over vegetable mixture. Toss.

Add peas and peaches. Toss gently. Makes 11 cups (2.75 L).

1 cup (250 mL): 91 Calories; 5.4 g Total Fat (2.4 g Mono, 1.8 g Poly, 0.9 g Sat); 0 mg Cholesterol; 10 g Carbohydrate; 2 g Fibre; 2 g Protein; 71 mg Sodium

Note: Wasabi peas are peas dry roasted in wasabi paste (Japanese horseradish). Available in Asian section of your local grocery store or an Asian grocery store.

 tip   *Instead of storing celery in paper or plastic bags, wrap in aluminum foil and place in refrigerator. When stored in this manner, celery will keep for weeks rather than days.*

Tortilla Jicama Salad

A wonderful combination of colours and textures. This Mexican-inspired dish is loaded with flavour and would go very well with a spicy main dish.

Julienned jicama	1 cup	250 mL
Head of romaine lettuce, cut or torn	1	1
Large avocados, sliced	2	2
Medium green pepper, thinly sliced	1	1
Halved cherry tomatoes	1 cup	250 mL
Thinly sliced red onion	1/2 cup	125 mL
CHILI DRESSING		
Cooking oil	1/4 cup	60 mL
Apple cider vinegar	2 tbsp.	30 mL
Garlic clove, minced (or 1/4 tsp., 1 mL, powder)	1	1
Hot pepper sauce	1/2 - 1 tsp.	2 - 5 mL
Chopped fresh oregano leaves (or 1/4 tsp., 1 mL, dried)	1 tsp.	5 mL
Ground cinnamon	1/4 tsp.	1 mL
Salt	1/4 tsp.	1 mL
Broken tortilla chips	1 cup	250 mL

Put first 6 ingredients into large bowl. Toss.

Chili Dressing: Combine first 7 ingredients in jar with tight-fitting lid. Shake well. Makes about 1/2 cup (125 mL) dressing. Drizzle over lettuce mixture. Toss gently.

Sprinkle with tortilla chips. Makes 16 cups (4 L).

1 cup (250 mL): 99 Calories; 8.3 g Total Fat (5 g Mono, 1.7 g Poly, 1 g Sat); 0 mg Cholesterol; 6 g Carbohydrate; 2 g Fibre; 1 g Protein; 60 mg Sodium

Pictured on page 71.

Date And Endive Salad

The exotic and attractive appearance of this salad is warmed by the presence of dates and toasted nuts. The blue cheese is subtle in the dressing.

Head of curly endive, cut or torn	1	1
Large pitted dates, sliced	1 cup	250 mL
Pine nuts, toasted (see Tip, page 86)	2/3 cup	150 mL
Medium pears, peeled and thinly sliced	2	2
BLUE CHEESE DRESSING		
Olive (or cooking) oil	3 tbsp.	50 mL
Crumbled blue cheese (about 1 oz., 28 g)	3 tbsp.	50 mL
White wine vinegar	2 tbsp.	30 mL
Granulated sugar	1 tsp.	5 mL

Put first 4 ingredients into large bowl. Toss gently.

Blue Cheese Dressing: Process all 4 ingredients in blender until smooth. Makes 1/3 cup (75 mL) dressing. Drizzle over endive mixture. Toss gently. Makes about 11 1/2 cups (2.9 L).

1 cup (250 mL): 153 Calories; 9.3 g Total Fat (4.7 g Mono, 2.4 g Poly, 1.7 g Sat); 2 mg Cholesterol; 18 g Carbohydrate; 3 g Fibre; 3 g Protein; 34 mg Sodium

Pictured on page 53.

Arugula And Pear Salad

Sweet slices of pear are the perfect complement to the peppery taste of arugula. You can use baby spinach in place of arugula if you prefer.

Trimmed arugula, packed	4 cups	1 L
Medium pear, peeled and thinly sliced	1	1
Salted cashews, coarsely chopped	1/3 cup	75 mL
Crumbled blue cheese (about 1 1/4 oz., 32 g)	1/4 cup	60 mL

(continued on next page)

BASIL DRESSING

Olive (or cooking) oil	3 tbsp.	50 mL
Red wine vinegar	2 tbsp.	30 mL
Coarsely chopped fresh sweet basil (or 1 1/2 tsp., 7 mL, dried)	2 tbsp.	30 mL
Liquid honey	1 tbsp.	15 mL

Put first 4 ingredients into large bowl. Toss.

Basil Dressing: Process all 4 ingredients in blender until smooth. Makes 1/3 cup (75 mL) dressing. Drizzle over arugula mixture. Toss. Makes 6 cups (1.5 L).

1 cup (250 mL): 150 Calories; 12.4 g Total Fat (7.7 g Mono, 1.3 g Poly, 2.8 g Sat); 5 mg Cholesterol; 9 g Carbohydrate; 1 g Fibre; 3 g Protein; 139 mg Sodium

Pictured on page 90.

Celery And Marshmallow Salad

Kids and adults alike will love this sweet, creamy salad. Marshmallows tossed with whipped cream give this crunchy salad a soft, fluffy appearance.

Whipping cream	1/2 cup	125 mL
Mayonnaise (not salad dressing)	3 tbsp.	50 mL
Chopped celery	3 cups	750 mL
Chopped green apple	1 1/2 cups	375 mL
Large marshmallows, quartered	20	20
Raisins	2/3 cup	150 mL
Pecans, toasted (see Tip, page 86) and coarsely chopped	1/2 cup	125 mL

Beat whipping cream in medium bowl until soft peaks form. Fold in mayonnaise.

Combine remaining 5 ingredients in large bowl. Fold in whipped cream mixture. Makes about 8 cups (2 L).

1 cup (250 mL): 254 Calories; 14.8 g Total Fat (7.1 g Mono, 2.9 g Poly, 4 g Sat); 21 mg Cholesterol; 32 g Carbohydrate; 2 g Fibre; 2 g Protein; 84 mg Sodium

Pineapple Lime Salad

An interesting blend of flavours with candied almonds,
peppery watercress, spicy curry powder and sweet chunks of pineapple.

Sliced almonds	1 1/3 cups	325 mL
Maple (or maple-flavoured) syrup	1/4 cup	60 mL
Curry powder	2 tsp.	10 mL
Trimmed watercress	5 cups	1.25 L
Can of pineapple chunks, drained	14 oz.	398 mL
Chopped green onion	1/3 cup	75 mL
LIME DRESSING		
Peanut (or cooking) oil	3 tbsp.	50 mL
Sour cream	2 tbsp.	30 mL
Lime juice	1 tbsp.	15 mL
Chili sauce	2 tsp.	10 mL
Salt	1/4 tsp.	1 mL
Coarsely ground pepper (or 1/8 tsp., 0.5 mL, pepper)	1/4 tsp.	1 mL

Combine almonds, maple syrup and curry powder in small bowl. Arrange in single layer on parchment paper-lined baking sheet. Bake in 375°F (190°C) oven for about 15 minutes, stirring once, until almonds are golden. Cool.

Arrange watercress in shallow serving dish. Top with pineapple and green onion. Sprinkle with almonds.

Lime Dressing: Combine all 6 ingredients in separate small bowl. Makes about 1/3 cup (75 mL) dressing. Drizzle over watercress mixture. Makes about 6 1/2 cups (1.6 L).

1 cup (250 mL): 260 Calories; 19.1 g Total Fat (10.9 g Mono, 4.6 g Poly, 2.6 g Sat); 2 mg Cholesterol; 20 g Carbohydrate; 4 g Fibre; 6 g Protein; 134 mg Sodium

Pictured on page 108.

Avocado And Bean Salad

A salad with an unusual, but yummy, combination of ingredients.
The delicious dressing is sure to spice up your life!

Shredded romaine lettuce	2 cups	500 mL
Can of black beans, rinsed and drained	14 oz.	398 mL
Chopped cucumber (with peel)	2 cups	500 mL
Chopped seeded tomato	1 cup	250 mL
Chopped red onion	2/3 cup	150 mL
JALAPEÑO DRESSING		
Olive (or cooking) oil	1/4 cup	60 mL
Lemon juice	3 tbsp.	50 mL
Chopped jalapeño pepper, seeds and ribs removed (see Note, below)	1 1/2 tbsp.	25 mL
Chopped fresh cilantro (or fresh parsley)	1 1/2 tbsp.	25 mL
Liquid honey	1 tbsp.	15 mL
Chili powder	1/4 – 1/2 tsp.	1 – 2 mL
Salt	1/4 tsp.	1 mL
Large avocados, chopped	2	2

Put first 5 ingredients into large bowl. Toss.

Jalapeño Dressing: Process first 7 ingredients in blender until smooth. Makes about 1/3 cup (75 mL) dressing. Drizzle over lettuce mixture. Toss.

Top with avocado. Makes about 10 cups (2.5 L).

1 cup (250 mL): 167 Calories; 12.2 g Total Fat (8.1 g Mono, 1.4 g Poly, 1.8 g Sat); 0 mg Cholesterol; 13 g Carbohydrate; 3 g Fibre; 4 g Protein; 123 mg Sodium

Note: Wear gloves when chopping jalapeño peppers and avoid touching your eyes.

Wasabi Pea Salad

*Your guests will love the unique and appealing colours and textures
of this salad. Adjust the amount of wasabi paste to suit your tastes.*

Sugar snap pea pods, trimmed	2 cups	500 mL
Boiling water		
Ice water		
Mixed salad greens	4 cups	1 L
Thinly sliced red onion	2/3 cup	150 mL
WASABI DRESSING		
Peanut (or cooking) oil	3 tbsp.	50 mL
Rice vinegar	2 tbsp.	30 mL
Soy sauce	1 tbsp.	15 mL
Brown sugar, packed	2 tsp.	10 mL
Wasabi paste (Japanese horseradish)	2 tsp.	10 mL
Dry chow mein noodles	2 cups	500 mL

Blanch pea pods in boiling water in medium saucepan for about 3 minutes
until bright green. Drain.

Plunge into ice water in large bowl. Let stand for 10 minutes until cold.
Drain. Put into salad bowl.

Add salad greens and onion. Toss.

Wasabi Dressing: Combine first 5 ingredients in jar with tight-fitting lid.
Shake well. Makes about 1/2 cup (125 mL) dressing. Drizzle over salad
green mixture.

Add noodles. Toss. Serve immediately. Makes about 8 cups (2 L).

*1 cup (250 mL): 125 Calories; 6 g Total Fat (2.5 g Mono, 1.8 g Poly, 1 g Sat); 10 mg Cholesterol;
15 g Carbohydrate; 2 g Fibre; 4 g Protein; 148 mg Sodium*

Pictured on page 36.

Paré Pointer
Barbers make good taxi drivers. They know all the shortcuts.

Marshmallow Greens Salad

The sweet marshmallows and fruit complement the bitter greens.
A pretty, leafy salad with bright red berries, soft chunks of
banana and a light, creamy dressing.

Cut or torn spinach, stems removed, lightly packed	3 cups	750 mL
Cut or torn curly endive, lightly packed	3 cups	750 mL
Thinly sliced red onion	1/3 cup	75 mL
LEMON POPPY SEED DRESSING		
Cooking oil	1/4 cup	60 mL
Lemon juice	3 tbsp.	50 mL
Liquid honey	3 tbsp.	50 mL
Apple cider vinegar	1 tbsp.	15 mL
Poppy seeds	1 tbsp.	15 mL
Pepper, sprinkle		
Miniature marshmallows	1 cup	250 mL
Sliced fresh strawberries	1/2 cup	125 mL
Medium banana, sliced	1	1

Put spinach, endive and onion into large bowl. Toss.

Lemon Poppy Seed Dressing: Process first 6 ingredients in blender for about 3 minutes until slightly thickened. Makes 2/3 cup (150 mL) dressing. Drizzle over spinach mixture. Toss.

Add marshmallows, strawberries and banana. Toss well to blend flavours. Makes 9 cups (2.25 L).

1 cup (250 mL): 127 Calories; 7.1 g Total Fat (3.9 g Mono, 2.3 g Poly, 0.6 g Sat); 0 mg Cholesterol; 17 g Carbohydrate; 1 g Fibre; 1 g Protein; 23 mg Sodium

 When purchasing curly endive, look for fresh, crisp heads with no discoloration or insect damage. Store heads in resealable freezer bag in refrigerator for up to 3 days.

Warm Lettuce Salad

This sweet, smoky dressing tastes so good on simple romaine greens.
Make the dressing right before serving so that it's still warm.

WARM BACON DRESSING

Apple cider vinegar	1/4 cup	60 mL
Granulated sugar	2 tbsp.	30 mL
Water	2 tbsp.	30 mL
Salt	1/2 tsp.	2 mL
Pepper	1/4 tsp.	1 mL
Bacon slices, diced	5	5
Chopped onion	1/2 cup	125 mL
Head of romaine lettuce, cut or torn	1	1
Green onions, chopped	3	3
Hard-boiled egg, chopped	1	1

Warm Bacon Dressing: Combine first 5 ingredients in jar with tight-fitting lid. Shake well.

Cook bacon and onion in frying pan until bacon is almost crisp. Spoon bacon, onion and drippings into same jar with tight-fitting lid. Shake well. Makes 1/2 cup (125 mL) dressing.

Put lettuce and green onion into large bowl. Drizzle with warm dressing. Toss.

Sprinkle with egg. Makes 6 cups (1.5 L).

1 cup (250 mL): 78 Calories; 3.7 g Total Fat (1.6 g Mono, 0.5 g Poly, 1.2 g Sat); 40 mg Cholesterol; 8 g Carbohydrate; 1 g Fibre; 4 g Protein; 299 mg Sodium

---

Paré Pointer
Cross a sheep with a kangaroo and you get a woolly jumper.

Spinach And Apricot Salad

Dried apricots add colour and an unusual sweetness to this salad. The delicious
peppercorn flavour of the dressing would go very well with a barbecued steak.

Spinach, stems removed, lightly packed	2 cups	500 mL
Heads of Belgian endive, leaves separated	2	2
Chopped dried apricot	1/2 cup	125 mL
Chopped green onion	1/3 cup	75 mL
Sunflower seeds, toasted (see Tip, page 86)	1/3 cup	75 mL
HERB AND PEPPERCORN DRESSING		
Peanut (or cooking) oil	3 tbsp.	50 mL
Chopped fresh chives (or 1 1/2 tsp., 7 mL, dried)	2 tbsp.	30 mL
Chopped fresh parsley (or 1 1/2 tsp., 7 mL, flakes)	2 tbsp.	30 mL
White wine vinegar	1 tbsp.	15 mL
Whole green peppercorns in brine, drained and finely chopped	1 tbsp.	15 mL
Paprika	1/2 tsp.	2 mL
Salt	1/4 tsp.	1 mL

Put first 5 ingredients into large bowl. Toss.

Herb And Peppercorn Dressing: Combine all 7 ingredients in jar with tight-fitting lid. Shake well. Makes about 1/3 cup (75 mL) dressing. Drizzle over spinach mixture. Toss. Makes about 6 cups (1.5 L).

1 cup (250 mL): 148 Calories; 11.5 g Total Fat (4.1 g Mono, 5.2 g Poly, 1.7 g Sat); 0 mg Cholesterol; 11 g Carbohydrate; 2 g Fibre; 3 g Protein; 138 mg Sodium

 tip *To store leafy greens, keep in refrigerator in paper, not plastic, bags. This will allow the leaves to breathe, preventing them from becoming soggy and limp.*

Ruby Chard And Raspberry Salad

The raspberry vinegar and orange zest in the dressing make this salad sensational! This will garner rave reviews from your guests.

Cut or torn ruby chard	6 cups	1.5 L
Fresh raspberries	1 cup	250 mL
Thinly sliced red onion	1/3 cup	75 mL
Coarsely crumbled goat (chèvre) cheese (about 1 1/2 oz., 43 g)	1/3 cup	75 mL
Pine nuts, toasted (see Tip, page 86)	1/3 cup	75 mL

RASPBERRY VINAIGRETTE

Fresh raspberries	1/4 cup	60 mL
Peanut (or cooking) oil	3 tbsp.	50 mL
Liquid honey	1 tbsp.	15 mL
Raspberry vinegar	1 tbsp.	15 mL
Finely grated orange zest	1/4 tsp.	1 mL
Salt	1/8 tsp.	0.5 mL
Coarsely ground pepper (or 1/16 tsp., 0.5 mL, pepper)	1/8 tsp.	0.5 mL

Put first 5 ingredients into large bowl. Toss gently.

Raspberry Vinaigrette: Process all 7 ingredients in blender until smooth. Strain through sieve, if desired. Makes about 2/3 cup (150 mL) dressing. Drizzle over chard mixture. Toss gently. Makes about 6 cups (1.5 L).

1 cup (250 mL): 176 Calories; 14.4 g Total Fat (5.6 g Mono, 4.3 g Poly, 3.7 g Sat); 7 mg Cholesterol; 10 g Carbohydrate; 3 g Fibre; 5 g Protein; 178 mg Sodium

Pictured on page 90.

 To toast nuts and seeds, arrange in single layer in ungreased shallow pan. Bake in 350°F (175°C) oven for 5 to 10 minutes, stirring or shaking often, until desired doneness.

Belgian Endive Salad

A tangy salad with pretty, pale Belgian endive leaves and eye-catching flecks of roasted red peppers.

Heads of Belgian endive, leaves separated	4	4
Jar of roasted red peppers, drained and chopped	13 oz.	370 mL
Chopped green onion	1/4 cup	60 mL
Coarsely grated fresh Parmesan cheese	1/4 cup	60 mL
Chopped fresh parsley (or 1 tbsp., 15 mL, flakes)	1/4 cup	60 mL
Head of green leaf lettuce, cut or torn	1	1
Hard-boiled eggs, coarsely chopped	3	3
Bacon slices, cooked crisp and crumbled	6	6
DIJON DRESSING		
Olive (or cooking) oil	1/4 cup	60 mL
Dijon mustard	2 tbsp.	30 mL
Mayonnaise (not salad dressing)	1 tbsp.	15 mL
Red wine vinegar	1 tbsp.	15 mL
Lemon juice	1 tbsp.	15 mL
Brown sugar, packed	1 tsp.	5 mL
Salt	1/4 tsp.	1 mL

Put first 8 ingredients into large bowl. Toss.

Dijon Dressing: Combine all 7 ingredients in jar with tight-fitting lid. Shake well. Makes about 1/2 cup (125 mL) dressing. Drizzle over vegetable mixture. Toss. Makes about 11 cups (2.75 L).

1 cup (250 mL): 130 Calories; 10.5 g Total Fat (6.1 g Mono, 1.4 g Poly, 2.4 g Sat); 64 mg Cholesterol; 5 g Carbohydrate; 1 g Fibre; 5 g Protein; 267 mg Sodium

---

Paré Pointer

That ocean resort was so lifeless and boring that when the tide went out it never came back.

Spinach And Blueberry Salad

A wonderful salad to make when blueberries are in season.
They add a hint of sweetness to the smoky bacon flavour.

Bag of spinach, stems removed	6 oz.	170 g
Fresh blueberries	1 cup	250 mL
Pecans, toasted (see Tip, page 86) and coarsely chopped	1/2 cup	125 mL
Bacon slices, cooked crisp and crumbled	6	6
PARMESAN DRESSING		
Olive (or cooking) oil	1/4 cup	60 mL
Finely grated fresh Parmesan cheese	3 tbsp.	50 mL
White wine vinegar	2 tbsp.	30 mL
Granulated sugar	1 tsp.	5 mL
Coarsely ground pepper (or 1/8 tsp., 0.5 mL, pepper)	1/4 tsp.	1 mL

Put first 4 ingredients into large bowl. Toss.

Parmesan Dressing: Process all 5 ingredients in blender until smooth. Makes about 1/3 cup (75 mL) dressing. Drizzle over spinach mixture. Toss. Makes about 10 cups (2.5 L).

1 cup (250 mL): 137 Calories; 12.5 g Total Fat (7.9 g Mono, 1.8 g Poly, 2.2 g Sat); 5 mg Cholesterol; 5 g Carbohydrate; 1 g Fibre; 3 g Protein; 111 mg Sodium

1. Tomato Basil Salad, page 24
2. Cucumber Avocado Salad, page 13

Props Courtesy Of: Cherison Enterprises Inc.

Orange And Watercress Salad

An attractive salad with a fantastic dressing. Your guests will love the look and the taste of this summery salad.

Trimmed watercress	6 cups	1.5 L
Medium oranges, peeled, cut crosswise into 1/4 inch (6 mm) thick slices and halved	2	2
Shaved fresh Parmesan cheese	1/4 cup	60 mL
HAZELNUT DRESSING		
White wine vinegar	2 tbsp.	30 mL
Cooking oil	2 tbsp.	30 mL
Hazelnut oil	2 tbsp.	30 mL
Garlic clove, minced (or 1/4 tsp., 1 mL, powder)	1	1
Hazelnuts (filberts), toasted (see Tip, page 86)	1/4 cup	60 mL

Put watercress, orange and cheese into large bowl. Toss.

Hazelnut Dressing: Process first 4 ingredients in blender until smooth.

Add hazelnuts. Process until hazelnuts are chopped. Do not overprocess. Makes 1/3 cup (75 mL) dressing. Drizzle over watercress mixture. Toss. Makes about 7 cups (1.75 L).

1 cup (250 mL): 137 Calories; 11.9 g Total Fat (7.9 g Mono, 1.9 g Poly, 1.5 g Sat); 3 mg Cholesterol; 6 g Carbohydrate; 2 g Fibre; 3 g Protein; 84 mg Sodium

1. Ruby Chard And Raspberry Salad, page 86
2. Asparagus In Tomato Butter, page 112
3. Arugula And Pear Salad, page 78
4. Strawberry Pecan Salad, page 25

Props Courtesy Of: Anchor Hocking Canada
Linens 'N Things
The Bay

Baby Bok Choy Noodle Salad

*Shanghai bok choy has light green ribs and leaves, a mild flavour
and a crisp texture. Toss with the delicious dressing for
an irresistible dish your family will devour!*

Bunch of Shanghai bok choy, trimmed, leaves and stems finely shredded	1	1
Chopped green onion	1/2 cup	125 mL
Can of sliced water chestnuts, drained	5 1/2 oz.	160 mL
PEANUT BUTTER DRESSING		
Peanut (or cooking) oil	6 tbsp.	100 mL
Rice vinegar	1/4 cup	60 mL
Smooth peanut butter	2 tbsp.	30 mL
Liquid honey	1 tbsp.	15 mL
Soy sauce	2 tsp.	10 mL
Chili paste (sambal oelek)	1/2 – 1 tsp.	2 – 5 mL
Dry chow mein noodles	2 cups	500 mL
Salted peanuts, coarsely chopped	2/3 cup	150 mL

Put bok choy, green onion and water chestnuts into large bowl. Toss.

Peanut Butter Dressing: Combine first 6 ingredients in jar with
tight-fitting lid. Shake well. Makes about 2/3 cup (150 mL) dressing.
Drizzle over bok choy mixture. Toss.

Add noodles and peanuts. Toss gently. Makes about 12 cups (3 L).

*1 cup (250 mL): 186 Calories; 13.1 g Total Fat (6.1 g Mono, 4.1 g Poly, 2.1 g Sat); 9 mg Cholesterol;
14 g Carbohydrate; 3 g Fibre; 5 g Protein; 238 mg Sodium*

Paré Pointer

*It's best not to break the law, but if you broke the law
of gravity, you'd likely get a suspended sentence.*

Asparagus And Tomato Salad

Beautiful dark asparagus pieces and bright red tomatoes are tossed with crispy bacon and feta cheese. The light dressing really brings out the flavour of the vegetables.

Fresh asparagus, trimmed of tough ends and cut into 2 inch (5 cm) pieces	2 lbs.	900 g
Boiling water		
Salt	1 tsp.	5 mL
Ice water		
Bacon slices, cooked crisp and crumbled	6	6
Medium tomatoes, quartered, seeded and chopped	2	2
Coarsely crumbled feta cheese (about 1 1/2 oz., 43 g)	1/3 cup	75 mL
Coarsely ground pepper (or 1/4 tsp., 1 mL, pepper)	1/2 tsp.	2 mL
LEMON DRESSING		
Lemon juice	2 tbsp.	30 mL
Olive (or cooking) oil	2 tbsp.	30 mL
Finely chopped fresh chives (or 1 1/2 tsp., 7 mL, dried)	2 tbsp.	30 mL
Finely chopped fresh parsley (or 1 1/2 tsp., 7 mL, flakes)	2 tbsp.	30 mL
Balsamic vinegar	1 tbsp.	15 mL
Granulated sugar	1 tsp.	5 mL
Salt	1/4 tsp.	1 mL

Cook asparagus in boiling water and salt in large saucepan for 3 to 5 minutes until bright green. Drain.

Plunge into ice water in large bowl. Let stand for 10 minutes until cold. Drain. Put into salad bowl.

Add next 4 ingredients. Toss.

Lemon Dressing: Combine all 7 ingredients in jar with tight-fitting lid. Shake well. Makes about 1/2 cup (125 mL) dressing. Drizzle over asparagus mixture. Toss. Makes about 6 cups (1.5 L).

1 cup (250 mL): 139 Calories; 10.1 g Total Fat (5.3 g Mono, 1 g Poly, 3.2 g Sat); 13 mg Cholesterol; 8 g Carbohydrate; 2 g Fibre; 6 g Protein; 317 mg Sodium

Grilled Pesto Vegetable Salad

Fresh, grilled vegetables are tossed with a flavourful pesto in this appetizing salad. Your guests will love the look and the taste of this dish.

Green peppers, quartered	2	2
Red peppers, quartered	2	2
Medium zucchini (with peel), cut lengthwise into 1/4 inch (6 mm) thick slices	3	3
Red onions, each cut into 8 wedges	2	2
SPINACH PESTO		
Spinach, stems removed, lightly packed	1 cup	250 mL
Pine nuts, toasted (see Tip, page 86)	1/4 cup	60 mL
Finely grated fresh Parmesan cheese	1/4 cup	60 mL
Olive (or cooking) oil	1/4 cup	60 mL
Balsamic vinegar	1 tbsp.	15 mL
Granulated sugar	1 tsp.	5 mL
Salt	1/4 tsp.	1 mL

Preheat gas barbecue to medium. Arrange green and red peppers, skin-side down, on greased grill. Cook for 10 to 15 minutes until skins are blistered and blackened. Remove to medium bowl. Cover with plastic wrap. Let sweat for about 15 minutes until cool enough to handle. Remove and discard skins. Cut into 1/2 inch (12 mm) wide strips. Put into large bowl.

Cook zucchini and onion on greased grill for 3 to 5 minutes per side until tender-crisp and grill marks appear. Add to peppers.

Spinach Pesto: Process all 7 ingredients in blender until smooth. Makes 2/3 cup (150 mL) dressing. Spoon over pepper mixture. Toss. Makes about 6 cups (1.5 L).

1 cup (250 mL): 203 Calories; 14.9 g Total Fat (8.8 g Mono, 2.6 g Poly, 2.8 g Sat); 3 mg Cholesterol; 15 g Carbohydrate; 5 g Fibre; 6 g Protein; 196 mg Sodium

Bean And Radicchio Salad

*The slightly bitter taste of radicchio is complemented by sweet,
fresh green beans and toasted macadamia nuts. A mild, green
olive dressing adds the finishing touch to this easy-to-prepare dish.*

Fresh green beans	1 1/2 lbs.	680 g
Boiling water		
Ice water		
Head of radicchio, trimmed and cut or torn	1	1
Macadamia nuts, toasted (see Tip, page 86) and coarsely chopped	1/2 cup	125 mL
OLIVE DRESSING		
Pimiento-stuffed olives	1/4 cup	60 mL
Olive (or cooking) oil	1/4 cup	60 mL
Lemon juice	1 tbsp.	15 mL
Granulated sugar	1 tsp.	5 mL
Pepper	1/8 tsp.	0.5 mL

Blanch green beans in boiling water in large saucepan for 3 to 5 minutes
until bright green. Drain.

Plunge into ice water in large bowl. Let stand for 10 minutes until cold.
Drain. Put into salad bowl.

Add radicchio and macadamia nuts. Toss.

Olive Dressing: Process all 5 ingredients in blender until smooth. Makes
1/2 cup (125 mL) dressing. Drizzle over radicchio mixture. Toss. Makes
about 12 cups (3 L).

*1 cup (250 mL): 111 Calories; 9.7 g Total Fat (7.3 g Mono, 0.6 g Poly, 1.4 g Sat); 0 mg Cholesterol;
6 g Carbohydrate; 2 g Fibre; 2 g Protein; 83 mg Sodium*

 *To clean fresh fiddleheads, gently rub them between your hands to
remove any loose or dry scales. Trim and discard ends and rinse
fiddleheads under water.*

Asparagus Yam Salad

An attractive, colourful salad with a hint of mint and sweet maple syrup in every bite.

Chopped yam (or sweet potato)	3 cups	750 mL
Olive (or cooking) oil	1 tbsp.	15 mL
Salt	1/4 tsp.	1 mL
Coarsely ground pepper (or 1/8 tsp., 0.5 mL, pepper)	1/4 tsp.	1 mL
Maple (or maple-flavoured) syrup	1 tbsp.	15 mL
Fresh asparagus, trimmed of tough ends and cut into 2 inch (5 cm) pieces	1 lb.	454 g
Boiling water		
Ice water		
Pecans, toasted (see Tip, page 86) and coarsely chopped	1/3 cup	75 mL
CHILI MINT DRESSING		
Coarsely chopped fresh mint leaves (or 2 1/4 tsp., 11 mL, dried)	3 tbsp.	50 mL
Olive (or cooking) oil	2 tbsp.	30 mL
Sweet (or regular) chili sauce	2 tbsp.	30 mL
White wine vinegar	1 tbsp.	15 mL
Salt	1/4 tsp.	1 mL

Put first 4 ingredients into large bowl. Toss. Arrange in single layer on greased baking sheet. Bake in 375°F (190°C) oven for 25 minutes, turning once.

Drizzle with maple syrup. Stir gently. Bake for about 15 minutes until browned. Put into same large bowl.

Blanch asparagus in boiling water in large saucepan for 3 to 5 minutes until bright green. Drain.

Plunge into ice water in large bowl. Let stand for 10 minutes until cold. Drain. Add to yam.

Add pecans. Toss.

Chili Mint Dressing: Process all 5 ingredients in blender until smooth. Makes 1/2 cup (125 mL) dressing. Drizzle over yam mixture. Toss. Makes about 4 cups (1 L).

1 cup (250 mL): 346 Calories; 17.7 g Total Fat (11.9 g Mono, 2.8 g Poly, 2.1 g Sat); 0 mg Cholesterol; 45 g Carbohydrate; 8 g Fibre; 5 g Protein; 426 mg Sodium

Pictured on page 107.

Creamy Fiddlehead Salad

A crunchy dish with fresh vegetables and fiddleheads
coated in a thick yogurt and mint dressing.

Fresh (or frozen, thawed) fiddleheads	3/4 lb.	340 g
Boiling water		
Salt	1 tsp.	5 mL
Ice water		
Thinly sliced English cucumber (with peel)	2 cups	500 mL
Thinly sliced red onion	1/2 cup	125 mL
CREAMY DRESSING		
Mayonnaise (not salad dressing)	3 tbsp.	50 mL
Plain yogurt	3 tbsp.	50 mL
Chopped fresh mint leaves (or 1 1/2 tsp., 7 mL, dried)	2 tbsp.	30 mL
Dijon mustard	2 tsp.	10 mL
Finely grated lemon zest	1/4 tsp.	1 mL
Salt	1/4 tsp.	1 mL
Coarsely ground pepper (or 1/8 tsp., 0.5 mL, pepper)	1/4 tsp.	1 mL

Cook fiddleheads in boiling water and salt in large saucepan for 3 to 5 minutes until bright green. Drain.

Plunge into ice water in large bowl. Let stand for 10 minutes until cold. Drain. Put into salad bowl.

Add cucumber and onion. Toss.

Creamy Dressing: Combine all 7 ingredients in small bowl. Makes 1/3 cup (75 mL) dressing. Spoon over fiddlehead mixture. Toss. Makes about 4 cups (1 L).

1 cup (250 mL): 120 Calories; 9.2 g Total Fat (4.8 g Mono, 3 g Poly, 1 g Sat); 7 mg Cholesterol; 7 g Carbohydrate; 2 g Fibre; 4 g Protein; 253 mg Sodium

Minted Pea Salad

A fresh mint dressing enhances this pretty salad.

Fresh (or frozen) peas	2 cups	500 mL
Water		
Broccoli florets	2 cups	500 mL
Boiling water		
Ice water		
Celery ribs, sliced	2	2
Jar of sliced pimiento, drained	2 oz.	57 mL
Medium onion, halved lengthwise	1	1
and sliced		
Small green pepper, slivered	1	1
MINT DRESSING		
Cooking oil	1/4 cup	60 mL
Lemon juice	2 tbsp.	30 mL
Coarsely chopped fresh mint leaves	2 tbsp.	30 mL
(or 1 1/2 tsp., 7 mL, dried)		
Granulated sugar	2 tsp.	10 mL
Salt	1/4 tsp.	1 mL
Pepper, sprinkle		

Cook peas in water in medium saucepan for about 2 minutes until barely tender. Do not overcook. Drain. Rinse under cold water. Drain. Put into large bowl.

Blanch broccoli in boiling water in same saucepan for 3 to 5 minutes until bright green. Drain.

Plunge into ice water in large bowl. Let stand for 10 minutes until cold. Drain. Add to peas.

Add next 4 ingredients. Toss.

Mint Dressing: Combine all 6 ingredients in small bowl. Makes about 1/3 cup (75 mL) dressing. Drizzle over broccoli mixture. Toss. Makes 6 cups (1.5 L).

1 cup (250 mL): 173 Calories; 10.1 g Total Fat (5.7 g Mono, 3.1 g Poly, 0.8 g Sat); 0 mg Cholesterol; 18 g Carbohydrate; 6 g Fibre; 5 g Protein; 129 mg Sodium

Pictured on page 126.

Beans With Garlic Crumbs

Garlic crumbs add crunch and a ton of flavour to this dish.
Toss with the delicious dressing and enjoy hot or cold.

Fresh green beans	1 lb.	454 g
Boiling water		
Ice water		
Olive (or cooking) oil	2 tbsp.	30 mL
Hard margarine (or butter)	1 tbsp.	15 mL
Garlic cloves, minced (or 1/2 tsp., 2 mL, powder)	2	2
Fresh bread crumbs	1 cup	250 mL
Chopped fresh parsley (or 3/4 tsp., 4 mL, flakes)	1 tbsp.	15 mL

SUN-DRIED TOMATO DRESSING

Olive (or cooking) oil	2 tbsp.	30 mL
Drained and chopped sun-dried tomatoes in oil	2 tbsp.	30 mL
Red wine vinegar	1 tbsp.	15 mL
Water	1 tbsp.	15 mL
Granulated sugar	1 tsp.	5 mL
Salt, sprinkle		

Blanch green beans in boiling water in large saucepan for 3 to 5 minutes until bright green. Drain.

Plunge into ice water in large bowl. Let stand for 10 minutes until cold. Drain. Place in large shallow dish or on large serving plate.

Heat olive oil and margarine in large frying pan on medium. Add garlic. Cook for about 1 minute, stirring constantly, until fragrant.

Add bread crumbs. Cook for about 5 minutes, stirring often, until crisp and golden.

Add parsley. Stir. Remove from heat.

Sun-Dried Tomato Dressing: Process all 6 ingredients in blender until smooth. Makes about 1/4 cup (60 mL) dressing. Drizzle over beans. Toss. Just before serving, sprinkle with bread crumb mixture. Toss. Makes 4 cups (1 L).

1 cup (250 mL): 312 Calories; 18.9 g Total Fat (12.9 g Mono, 2.1 g Poly, 2.9 g Sat); 0 mg Cholesterol; 32 g Carbohydrate; 4 g Fibre; 6 g Protein; 293 mg Sodium

Vegetable Salads

Green Bean Salad

Bright garden vegetables are tossed in a tangy, refreshing vinaigrette.
A crisp, light dish that is best served fresh.

Fresh (or frozen, thawed) french-cut green beans (about 4 1/2 cups, 1.1 L)	1 lb.	454 g
Boiling water		
Ice water		
Fresh (or frozen) peas (about 3 1/2 cups, 875 mL)	1 lb.	454 g
Water		
Small onion, thinly sliced	1	1
Sliced celery	1 cup	250 mL
Jar of sliced pimiento, drained	2 oz.	57 mL
VINAIGRETTE		
Granulated sugar	1 cup	250 mL
White vinegar	1 cup	250 mL
Cooking oil	1/4 cup	60 mL
Mustard seed (or dry mustard)	1/2 tsp.	2 mL
Salt	1/4 tsp.	1 mL

Blanch green beans in boiling water in medium saucepan for 3 to 5 minutes until bright green. Drain.

Plunge into ice water in large bowl. Let stand for 10 minutes until cold. Drain. Put into salad bowl.

Cook peas in water in same saucepan for about 2 minutes until barely tender. Do not overcook. Drain. Rinse under cold water. Drain well. Add to beans.

Add onion, celery and pimiento.

Vinaigrette: Process all 5 ingredients in blender until sugar is dissolved. Makes 2 cups (500 mL) dressing. Drizzle over vegetable mixture. Toss. Makes about 7 1/2 cups (1.9 L).

1 cup (250 mL): 270 Calories; 8.2 g Total Fat (4.6 g Mono, 2.5 g Poly, 0.6 g Sat); 0 mg Cholesterol; 47 g Carbohydrate; 2 g Fibre; 6 g Protein; 103 mg Sodium

Note: To make ahead, press salad down so dressing covers vegetables fairly well. Cover. Can be stored in refrigerator for up to 72 hours. (The bright green colours will dull, but the flavour will stay the same.) Remove vegetable mixture to serving dish with slotted spoon.

Cucumber And Couscous Sa'

*A lively salad with a wonderful combination of sweet and spicy ingredien...
Crunchy cucumber and soft dates texture this zesty dish.
Serve on a bed of lettuce.*

Couscous	1 cup	250 mL
Boiling water	1 cup	250 mL
Olive (or cooking) oil	1 tbsp.	15 mL
Salt	1/4 tsp.	1 mL
Chopped cucumber (with peel)	2 cups	500 mL
Coarsely grated zucchini (with peel)	1 cup	250 mL
Chopped dates	2/3 cup	150 mL
Chopped green onion	1/2 cup	125 mL
Chopped fresh mint leaves (or 3/4 – 2 1/4 tsp., 4 – 11 mL, dried)	1 – 3 tbsp.	15 – 50 mL

CHILI DRESSING

Olive (or cooking) oil	1/4 cup	60 mL
White wine vinegar	2 tbsp.	30 mL
Liquid honey	1 tbsp.	15 mL
Chili powder	1/2 tsp.	2 mL
Salt	1/4 tsp.	1 mL
Coarsely ground pepper (or 1/8 tsp., 0.5 mL, pepper)	1/4 tsp.	1 mL

Put first 4 ingredients into large bowl. Stir. Cover. Let stand for 5 minutes. Fluff with fork.

Add next 5 ingredients. Toss.

Chili Dressing: Combine all 6 ingredients in jar with tight-fitting lid. Shake well. Makes 1/2 cup (125 mL) dressing. Drizzle over cucumber mixture. Toss. Makes about 5 cups (1.25 L).

1 cup (250 mL): 369 Calories; 14.8 g Total Fat (10.5 g Mono, 1.4 g Poly, 2 g Sat); 0 mg Cholesterol; 56 g Carbohydrate; 5 g Fibre; 6 g Protein; 248 mg Sodium

Pictured on page 54.

Asparagus Blueberry Mold

This salad is so pretty with asparagus and blueberries peeking through clear lemon jelly. This is a unique salad that your guests will long remember. A bundt pan works very well as a mold.

Packages of lemon-flavoured jelly powder (gelatin), 3 oz. (85 g) each	2	2
Boiling water	1 1/2 cups	375 mL
Cold water	1 cup	250 mL
Lemon juice	2 tbsp.	30 mL
Fresh asparagus, trimmed of tough ends and cut into 1 inch (2.5 cm) pieces	8 oz.	225 g
Boiling water		
Ice water		
Fresh (or frozen, thawed) blueberries	1 cup	250 mL
Chopped pecans, toasted (see Tip, page 86)	1/4 cup	60 mL

Dissolve jelly powder in first amount of boiling water in medium bowl.

Stir in cold water and lemon juice. Chill for about 1 1/4 hours, stirring and scraping down side of bowl several times, until slightly thickened.

Blanch asparagus in boiling water in medium saucepan for 3 to 5 minutes until bright green. Drain.

Plunge into ice water in large bowl. Let stand for 10 minutes until cold. Drain.

Fold asparagus, blueberries and pecans into gelatin mixture. Pour into 5 to 6 cup (1.25 to 1.5 L) mold. Cover with plastic wrap. Chill for several hours or overnight until set. Makes 4 1/2 cups (1.1 L).

2/3 cup (150 mL): 136 Calories; 3 g Total Fat (1.8 g Mono, 0.7 g Poly, 0.2 g Sat); 0 mg Cholesterol; 26 g Carbohydrate; 1 g Fibre; 3 g Protein; 61 mg Sodium

 To remove a jellied salad from its mold, dip the mold into very warm water for about 10 seconds. Gently pull edge of salad away from mold with your fingertips. Invert large plate over mold and then, holding them together, turn over. Gently shake back and forth until salad loosens. Repeat steps if necessary. Carefully remove mold.

The Best Broccoli Salad

*You've probably tasted this popular salad many
times and wanted the recipe. Well, here it is!*

Bacon slices, finely diced	10	10
Large head of broccoli, cut into florets, stems peeled and chopped (about 1 1/2 lbs., 680 g)	1	1
Small red onion, halved lengthwise and thinly sliced	1	1
Golden raisins	1 cup	250 mL
DRESSING		
Mayonnaise (not salad dressing)	1 cup	250 mL
Granulated sugar	1/4 cup	60 mL
White vinegar	2 tbsp.	30 mL
Chopped dried chives	2 tsp.	10 mL
Salted sunflower seeds, toasted (see Tip, page 86)	2/3 cup	150 mL

Cook bacon in large frying pan until almost crisp. Remove to paper towel to drain. Put into large bowl.

Add broccoli, onion and raisins. Toss.

Dressing: Combine first 4 ingredients in small bowl. Let stand for about 5 minutes until sugar is dissolved. Stir. Makes about 1 1/3 cups (325 mL) dressing. Drizzle over broccoli mixture. Toss.

Just before serving, sprinkle with sunflower seeds. Toss or serve as is. Makes 12 cups (3 L).

*1 cup (250 mL): 290 Calories; 22.2 g Total Fat (10.6 g Mono, 8.1 g Poly, 2.8 g Sat);
16 mg Cholesterol; 20 g Carbohydrate; 3 g Fibre; 5 g Protein; 261 mg Sodium*

Paré Pointer

*Have you ever noticed that there are two kinds
of parking in the city? Illegal and occupied.*

Sweet Cabbage Salad

A shredded cabbage dish with sweet, chewy raisins and soft cubes
of cheese. This salad appeals to the eye and to the palate.

Shredded cabbage	4 cups	1 L
Grated carrot	1 cup	250 mL
Diced medium (or sharp) Cheddar cheese	1 cup	250 mL
Apple (your choice), peeled and grated	1	1
Dark raisins	1/2 cup	125 mL
DRESSING		
Granulated sugar	1/4 cup	60 mL
White vinegar	2 tbsp.	30 mL
Cooking oil	2 tbsp.	30 mL
Lemon juice	1 tbsp.	15 mL

Put first 5 ingredients into large bowl. Toss.

Dressing: Put all 4 ingredients into small bowl. Stir for 2 to 3 minutes until sugar is dissolved. Drizzle over cabbage mixture. Toss. Makes 7 cups (1.75 L).

1 cup (250 mL): 200 Calories; 9.9 g Total Fat (3.9 g Mono, 1.4 g Poly, 3.9 g Sat); 18 mg Cholesterol; 25 g Carbohydrate; 2 g Fibre; 5 g Protein; 121 mg Sodium

Hot Apple Slaw

A warm, pale green mix of cabbage and apple tossed in a sweet vinaigrette.
Leftovers can easily be stir-fried to make a hot, tasty side dish.

Shredded cabbage	4 cups	1 L
Water	1/4 cup	60 mL
Brown sugar, packed	1/4 cup	60 mL
White vinegar	3 tbsp.	50 mL
Salt	1 tsp.	5 mL
Dill weed	1/4 tsp.	1 mL
Medium cooking apples (such as McIntosh), with peel, finely chopped	2	2

(continued on next page)

Vegetable Salads

Put cabbage into medium bowl.

Combine next 5 ingredients in small saucepan. Bring to a boil. Heat and stir until brown sugar is dissolved. Remove from heat.

Add apple. Stir. Let stand for 1 minute. Drizzle over cabbage. Toss. Makes about 5 cups (1.25 L).

1 cup (250 mL): 93 Calories; 0.4 g Total Fat (trace Mono, 0.1 g Poly, 0.1 g Sat); 0 mg Cholesterol; 24 g Carbohydrate; 2 g Fibre; 1 g Protein; 490 mg Sodium

STIR-FRIED CABBAGE SIDE DISH: Heat small amount of cooking oil in wok or large frying pan on medium-high. Add leftover Hot Apple Slaw, stirring constantly, until heated through.

Broccoli Orange Salad

This salad is infused with a sweet, smoky flavour. The bright segments of orange contrast the green broccoli for a pleasing presentation.

Bacon slices, cooked crisp and crumbled	5	5
Cans of mandarin orange segments (10 oz., 284 mL, each), drained	2	2
Large head of broccoli, cut into florets, stems peeled and chopped (about 1 1/2 lbs., 680 g)	1	1
Finely chopped red (or white) onion	1/2 cup	125 mL
Chopped pecans (or walnuts), toasted (see Tip, page 86)	1/2 cup	125 mL
DRESSING		
Mayonnaise (not salad dressing)	1 cup	250 mL
Granulated sugar	1/4 cup	60 mL
Apple cider vinegar	3 tbsp.	50 mL
Ketchup	1 1/2 tsp.	7 mL

Put first 5 ingredients into large bowl. Toss.

Dressing: Combine all 4 ingredients in small bowl. Let stand for about 5 minutes until sugar is dissolved. Stir. Makes about 1 1/3 cups (325 mL) dressing. Drizzle over broccoli mixture. Toss. Makes 8 cups (2 L).

1 cup (250 mL): 370 Calories; 30.9 g Total Fat (17.2 g Mono, 9.5 g Poly, 3.4 g Sat); 21 mg Cholesterol; 22 g Carbohydrate; 3 g Fibre; 5 g Protein; 252 mg Sodium

Crunchy Pea Salad

Perfectly cooked pasta is coated in a golden sauce and tossed with light, fresh vegetables. You'll love the crunchy texture and the mild heat in the aftertaste.

Cooked penne pasta (about 1 cup, 250 mL, uncooked)	2 cups	500 mL
Thinly sliced green pepper	1 1/2 cups	375 mL
Julienned fresh pea pods	1 1/2 cups	375 mL
Coarsely grated carrot	1 cup	250 mL
Finely chopped red onion	2/3 cup	150 mL
Slivered almonds, toasted (see Tip, page 86)	1/2 cup	125 mL
DRESSING		
Olive (or cooking) oil	1/4 cup	60 mL
Rice vinegar	3 tbsp.	50 mL
Soy sauce	1 tbsp.	15 mL
Liquid honey	1 tbsp.	15 mL
Chili paste (sambal oelek)	1 tsp.	5 mL
Garlic salt	1/2 tsp.	2 mL

Put first 6 ingredients into large bowl. Toss.

Dressing: Combine all 6 ingredients in jar with tight-fitting lid. Shake well. Makes 2/3 cup (150 mL) dressing. Drizzle over pasta mixture. Toss. Makes about 8 cups (2 L).

1 cup (250 mL): 259 Calories; 12.3 g Total Fat (8.3 g Mono, 1.8 g Poly, 1.5 g Sat); 0 mg Cholesterol; 32 g Carbohydrate; 3 g Fibre; 7 g Protein; 215 mg Sodium

1. Asparagus Yam Salad, page 96
2. Toffee Nut And Spinach Salad, page 68
3. Cranberry Brie Salad, page 67

Props Courtesy Of: Casa Bugatti
Pier 1 Imports
The Bay

Vegetable Salads

Cucumber Mango Salad

Fresh mangoes, lime juice and macadamia nuts give this colourful, sweet and spicy salad a tropical feel. Yum!

English cucumber (with peel), thinly sliced	1	1
Chopped (or canned, drained) mango	1 cup	250 mL
Macadamia nuts, toasted (see Tip, page 86) and coarsely chopped	1/2 cup	125 mL
CILANTRO LIME DRESSING		
Lime juice	2 tbsp.	30 mL
Peanut (or cooking) oil	2 tbsp.	30 mL
Finely chopped fresh cilantro (or fresh parsley)	1 tbsp.	15 mL
Sweet (or regular) chili sauce	1 tbsp.	15 mL
Dried crushed chilies	1/2 tsp.	2 mL
Salt	1/4 tsp.	1 mL

Put cucumber, mango and macadamia nuts into medium bowl. Toss.

Cilantro Lime Dressing: Combine all 6 ingredients in jar with tight-fitting lid. Shake well. Makes about 1/3 cup (75 mL) dressing. Drizzle over cucumber mixture. Toss. Makes 4 cups (1 L).

1 cup (250 mL): 232 Calories; 20.2 g Total Fat (13.5 g Mono, 2.5 g Poly, 3.2 g Sat); 0 mg Cholesterol; 14 g Carbohydrate; 4 g Fibre; 3 g Protein; 214 mg Sodium

1. Pineapple Lime Salad, page 80
2. Coleslaw With Shrimp Crisps, page 14

Props Courtesy Of: La Cache

Green Onion Rice

This tasty dish is sure to be a hit! Caramelized green onions are combined with fragrant jasmine rice and a touch of spice.

Water	3/4 cup	175 mL
Jasmine rice	1/2 cup	125 mL
Salt	1/4 tsp.	1 mL
Peanut (or cooking) oil	1 tbsp.	15 mL
Chopped green onion (cut into 1/2 inch, 12 mm, pieces)	3 cups	750 mL
Garlic cloves, minced (or 1/2 tsp., 2 mL, powder)	2	2
Chili paste (sambal oelek)	1/2 – 1 tsp.	2 – 5 mL
Rice vinegar	1 1/2 tbsp.	25 mL
Granulated sugar	1 1/2 tbsp.	25 mL
Salt	1/4 tsp.	1 mL
Coarsely chopped salted peanuts	1/2 cup	125 mL

Put water into small saucepan. Bring to a boil. Add rice and first amount of salt. Stir. Cover. Simmer on low for 15 minutes. Remove from heat. Do not lift lid. Let stand for 5 minutes. Fluff with fork. Keep warm.

Heat peanut oil in large frying pan on medium-low. Add green onion, garlic and chili paste. Cook for 7 to 10 minutes, stirring occasionally, until green onion is soft.

Add vinegar, sugar and second amount of salt. Stir until well combined.

Add rice and peanuts. Heat and stir until hot. Makes about 3 cups (750 mL).

1/2 cup (125 mL): 169 Calories; 7.5 g Total Fat (3.6 g Mono, 2.4 g Poly, 1.1 g Sat); 0 mg Cholesterol; 23 g Carbohydrate; 2 g Fibre; 5 g Protein; 289 mg Sodium

Creamy Pattypan Squash

A wonderful combination of colours and flavours. This would
go so well with roasted meat and mashed potatoes.

Green pattypan squash, cut into 1/3 inch (1 cm) thick slices	1 1/2 lbs.	680 g
Water		
Cooking oil	2 tsp.	10 mL
Finely chopped onion	1/3 cup	75 mL
Garlic clove, minced (or 1/4 tsp., 1 mL, powder)	1	1
Sour cream	1/3 cup	75 mL
Honey mustard	2 tbsp.	30 mL
Chopped fresh dill (or 1/2 tsp., 2 mL, dill weed)	2 tsp.	10 mL
Salt	1/4 tsp.	1 mL
Pepper	1/4 tsp.	1 mL

Cook squash in water in large saucepan for 3 to 5 minutes until tender-crisp. Drain.

Heat cooking oil in large frying pan on medium-low. Add onion and garlic. Cook for about 5 minutes, stirring occasionally, until onion is soft.

Add remaining 5 ingredients. Heat and stir until hot. Add squash. Stir until coated. Makes about 4 cups (1 L).

1/2 cup (125 mL): 56 Calories; 2.9 g Total Fat (1.2 g Mono, 0.5 g Poly, 1 g Sat); 4 mg Cholesterol; 7 g Carbohydrate; 2 g Fibre; 2 g Protein; 106 mg Sodium

Paré Pointer
When their canary was a year old they gave it a birdy party.

Asparagus In Tomato Butter

This dish is easy to prepare and is full of complementary flavours.
Sweet sun-dried tomatoes and basil add colour and interest
to the tender, green asparagus spears.

TOMATO BUTTER

Olive (or cooking) oil	2 tsp.	10 mL
Finely chopped red onion	1/3 cup	75 mL
Lemon juice	1 tsp.	5 mL
Butter (or hard margarine), softened	1/4 cup	60 mL
Chopped sun-dried tomatoes in oil, drained	3 tbsp.	50 mL
Chopped fresh sweet basil (or 3/4 tsp., 4 mL, dried)	1 tbsp.	15 mL
Fresh asparagus, trimmed of tough ends	1 lb.	454 g
Water		

Tomato Butter: Heat olive oil in small frying pan on medium-low. Add onion. Cook for about 5 minutes, stirring occasionally, until onion is soft. Cool. Put into shallow serving dish.

Add next 4 ingredients to onion. Stir well. Makes 1/2 cup (125 mL) butter.

Cook asparagus in water in large saucepan for 3 to 5 minutes until tender-crisp. Add asparagus to butter mixture. Toss. Serves 4.

1 serving: 168 Calories; 15.5 g Total Fat (5.7 g Mono, 0.9 g Poly, 8.1 g Sat); 33 mg Cholesterol; 7 g Carbohydrate; 2 g Fibre; 3 g Protein; 141 mg Sodium

Pictured on page 90.

 To trim tough ends from asparagus spears, hold bottom of spear with one hand and just under tip with other hand. Bend stalk until it snaps and breaks at the point where toughness ends.

Zucchini Clusters

Spiky bundles of golden zucchini and bright green strips of peel in this fun side dish. These are best served fresh when the batter is still delightfully crisp.

All-purpose flour	2/3 cup	150 mL
Cornstarch	3 tbsp.	50 mL
Cornmeal	3 tbsp.	50 mL
Seasoned salt	1 tsp.	5 mL
Granulated sugar	1 tsp.	5 mL
Salt	1/4 tsp.	1 mL
Egg whites (large), fork-beaten	3	3
Ice water	1/3 cup	75 mL
Medium zucchini (with peel), cut julienne	4	4

Cooking oil, for deep-frying

Salt, sprinkle

Combine first 6 ingredients in large bowl.

Add egg whites and ice water. Stir with whisk to remove any lumps. Add zucchini, 1/4 cup (60 mL) at a time, to batter for each cluster. Remove each cluster with slotted spoon.

Deep-fry in hot (375°F, 190°C) cooking oil for about 5 minutes until golden brown. Remove to paper towels to drain.

Sprinkle with second amount of salt. Makes 16 to 18 clusters.

1 cluster: 83 Calories; 4.8 g Total Fat (2.7 g Mono, 1.4 g Poly, 0.4 g Sat); 0 mg Cholesterol; 8 g Carbohydrate; 1 g Fibre; 2 g Protein; 86 mg Sodium

Pictured on page 143.

Paré Pointer
Cross a galaxy with a toad and you get star warts.

Coconut Chinese Broccoli

Also known as "gai lum" or "Chinese kale," Chinese broccoli has slightly waxy leaves and stems which are light to medium green in colour. The smooth, sweet coconut sauce is the perfect complement to the crisp, green broccoli.

Cooking oil	2 tsp.	10 mL
Garlic clove, minced (or 1/4 tsp., 1 mL, powder)	1	1
Coconut milk	2/3 cup	150 mL
Sweet (or regular) chili sauce	3 tbsp.	50 mL
Soy sauce	1 tbsp.	15 mL
Coarsely chopped Chinese broccoli (with stalks), about 1 bunch	6 cups	1.5 L
Flake coconut, toasted (see Tip, page 86)	3 tbsp.	50 mL

Heat cooking oil in wok or large frying pan on medium. Add garlic. Stir-fry for about 1 minute until fragrant.

Add next 3 ingredients. Stir until boiling.

Add broccoli. Stir. Cover. Cook for 5 to 10 minutes until stalks are tender-crisp.

Sprinkle with coconut. Makes about 4 cups (1 L).

1/2 cup (125 mL): 93 Calories; 7.1 g Total Fat (0.9 g Mono, 0.5 g Poly, 5.2 g Sat); 0 mg Cholesterol; 7 g Carbohydrate; 2 g Fibre; 3 g Protein; 240 mg Sodium

Baby Bok Choy Side Dish

This tender-crisp baby bok choy is drizzled with a glossy ginger glaze. Make sure you rinse the stalks very well to remove any dirt that may be trapped in the base. Before you begin eating, remove the root ends from the stalks, or simply eat around them.

Stalks of baby bok choy (about 3/4 – 1 lb., 340 – 454 g)	6	6
Water		

(continued on next page)

114 Side Dishes

Hard margarine (or butter)	1 tbsp.	15 mL
Minced crystallized ginger	1 1/2 tsp.	7 mL
Sliced green onion	2 tbsp.	30 mL
Oyster sauce	3 tbsp.	50 mL

Cook bok choy in water in Dutch oven for 2 to 3 minutes until base is tender-crisp. Drain well. Keep warm.

Melt margarine in small saucepan on medium. Add ginger and green onion. Cook for 1 to 2 minutes, stirring often, until green onion is soft.

Add oyster sauce. Heat and stir until hot. Pour over bok choy. Toss gently. Serves 6.

1 serving: 36 Calories; 2.1 g Total Fat (1.3 g Mono, 0.3 g Poly, 0.5 g Sat); trace Cholesterol; 4 g Carbohydrate; 1 g Fibre; 1 g Protein; 802 mg Sodium

Cabbage Stir-Fry

An easy-to-make cabbage side dish coated in a glistening glaze.
You'll delight in the subtle flavours and the slight heat in the aftertaste.

Peanut (or cooking) oil	1 tbsp.	15 mL
Hard margarine (or butter)	2 tbsp.	30 mL
Chopped green onion	1/3 cup	75 mL
Garlic clove, minced (or 1/4 tsp., 1 mL, powder)	1	1
Shredded cabbage	8 cups	2 L
Apple cider vinegar	2 tbsp.	30 mL
Brown sugar, packed	1 tbsp.	15 mL
Salt	1/4 – 1/2 tsp.	1 – 2 mL
Pepper	1/8 – 1/4 tsp.	0.5 – 1 mL

Heat peanut oil and margarine in wok or large frying pan on medium-high. Add green onion and garlic. Stir-fry for about 1 minute until fragrant.

Add remaining 5 ingredients. Stir-fry for about 3 minutes until cabbage is tender-crisp. Makes about 6 cups (1.5 L).

1/2 cup (125 mL): 46 Calories; 3.2 g Total Fat (1.8 g Mono, 0.6 g Poly, 0.6 g Sat); 0 mg Cholesterol; 4 g Carbohydrate; 1 g Fibre; 1 g Protein; 82 mg Sodium

Celery And Fennel Bake

A wonderful, aromatic dish to make between fall and spring when fennel and celery are both in season.

Celery ribs, trimmed and halved crosswise	6	6
Water		
Fennel bulb (white part only), thinly sliced	1	1
Hard margarine (or butter), melted	2 tbsp.	30 mL
Olive (or cooking) oil	1 tbsp.	15 mL
Finely chopped onion	1/2 cup	125 mL
Garlic cloves, minced (or 1/2 tsp., 2 mL, powder)	2	2
Roma (plum) tomatoes, chopped	4	4
Balsamic vinegar	1 tbsp.	15 mL
Granulated sugar	1 tsp.	5 mL
Salt	1/4 tsp.	1 mL
Finely grated fresh Parmesan cheese	1/3 cup	75 mL

Cook celery in water in large pot or Dutch oven for 10 minutes. Drain well.

Layer celery and fennel in greased shallow 2 quart (2 L) casserole.

Heat margarine and olive oil in medium frying pan on medium. Add onion and garlic. Cook for about 5 minutes, stirring often, until onion is soft.

Add next 4 ingredients. Stir. Pour over celery mixture. Stir gently to coat. Cover. Bake in 375°F (190°C) oven for 35 minutes. Remove cover.

Sprinkle with cheese. Bake, uncovered, for about 20 minutes until celery and fennel are tender and cheese is golden. Makes 4 cups (1 L).

1/2 cup (125 mL): 91 Calories; 6.2 g Total Fat (3.6 g Mono, 0.6 g Poly, 1.7 g Sat); 3 mg Cholesterol; 7 g Carbohydrate; 1 g Fibre; 3 g Protein; 213 mg Sodium

Fried Okra

Crunchy-looking rolls dipped in egg and coated in a warm
cornmeal crust. You'll love these even if you think you don't like okra!

Large egg	1	1
Water	1 tbsp.	15 mL
Fresh okra (with peel), cut into 1 inch (2.5 cm) pieces (about 3 1/2 cups, 875 mL)	1 lb.	454 g
Cornmeal	2/3 cup	150 mL
All-purpose flour	1/4 cup	60 mL
Salt	1 1/4 tsp.	6 mL
Chili powder	1 1/4 tsp.	6 mL
Cayenne pepper	1/4 – 1/2 tsp.	1 – 2 mL

Cooking oil, for deep-frying

Beat egg and water with fork in medium bowl.

Add okra. Stir until coated.

Combine next 5 ingredients in shallow dish. Coat several pieces of okra at a time in cornmeal mixture.

Deep-fry, in batches, in hot (375°F, 190°C) cooking oil for about 4 minutes until golden. Remove to paper towels to drain. Makes about 3 cups (750 mL).

1/2 cup (125 mL): 208 Calories; 11 g Total Fat (6.1 g Mono, 3.1 g Poly, 1 g Sat); 36 mg Cholesterol; 23 g Carbohydrate; 4 g Fibre; 5 g Protein; 517 mg Sodium

tip *To maintain optimum flavour, store tomatoes at room temperature. Refrigeration will stop the ripening process and alter flavour and texture.*

Devilled Peas

A rich, cheesy sauce surrounds sweet green peas
in this comforting baked dish.

Fresh cooked (or frozen, thawed) peas	3 cups	750 mL
Can of condensed cream of mushroom soup	10 oz.	284 mL
Chili sauce (or ketchup)	2 tbsp.	30 mL
Milk	2 tbsp.	30 mL
Worcestershire sauce	1 1/2 tsp.	7 mL
Hard-boiled eggs, sliced	3	3
Grated medium Cheddar cheese	1 cup	250 mL
TOPPING		
Hard margarine (or butter)	2 tbsp.	30 mL
Buttery cracker crumbs	1/2 cup	125 mL

Layer peas evenly in bottom of ungreased 1 1/2 quart (1.5 L) casserole.

Combine next 4 ingredients in small bowl. Spoon over peas. Spread evenly.

Layer egg on top. Sprinkle with cheese.

Topping: Melt margarine in small saucepan. Stir in cracker crumbs. Sprinkle over cheese. Bake, uncovered, in 350°F (175°C) oven for about 45 minutes until hot and bubbly. Makes 4 cups (1 L).

1/2 cup (125 mL): 250 Calories; 14.7 g Total Fat (5.4 g Mono, 2.7 g Poly, 5.5 g Sat); 97 mg Cholesterol; 19 g Carbohydrate; 5 g Fibre; 11 g Protein; 589 mg Sodium

Pictured on page 126.

Paré Pointer
Do you realize what shape the world is in? It's round.

Orange Hazelnut Broccoli

*This dish is so quick and easy to make! You can substitute
the hazelnuts with any nuts of your choice.*

Orange juice	3 tbsp.	50 mL
Hard margarine (or butter)	2 tbsp.	30 mL
Liquid honey	1 tbsp.	15 mL
Dijon mustard	2 tsp.	10 mL
Finely grated orange zest	1/4 tsp.	1 mL
Broccoli florets	5 cups	1.25 L
Water		
Salt, just a pinch		
Hazelnuts (filberts), toasted (see Tip, page 86) and coarsely chopped	1/4 cup	60 mL

Put first 5 ingredients into small saucepan. Heat and stir on medium until margarine is melted. Boil gently, without stirring, for about 2 minutes until thickened.

Cook broccoli in water and salt in large saucepan for about 5 minutes until tender-crisp. Drain well. Add orange juice mixture. Stir until coated.

Sprinkle with hazelnuts. Stir. Makes about 4 cups (1 L).

1/2 cup (125 mL): 78 Calories; 5.6 g Total Fat (3.8 g Mono, 0.7 g Poly, 0.8 g Sat); 0 mg Cholesterol; 7 g Carbohydrate; 2 g Fibre; 2 g Protein; 70 mg Sodium

 To score a cucumber, drag a fork, using even amount of pressure, lengthwise down the skin. Repeat this process all the way around the cucumber. Scoring creates a pretty effect when the cucumber is sliced as there are alternating strips of skin and flesh on the outside.

Artichoke And Tomato

Smoky bacon is blended into sweet tomatoes, basil and a touch of
wine to create an absolutely delicious combination of flavours.
This would be perfect with pasta, fish or chicken.

Medium globe artichokes	4	4
Lemon juice	2 tbsp.	30 mL
Boiling water		
Bacon slices, cut into 1 inch (2.5 cm) pieces	8	8
Chopped onion	1 cup	250 mL
Garlic cloves, minced (or 1/2 tsp., 2 mL, powder)	2	2
Dry white (or alcohol-free) wine	1/4 cup	60 mL
Can of diced tomatoes (with juice)	14 oz.	398 mL
Pepper	1/4 tsp.	1 mL
Chopped fresh sweet basil (or 1 1/2 tsp., 7 mL, dried)	2 tbsp.	30 mL

Cut stems off artichokes. Cut about 1/3 off top. Cut prickly tips off all
leaves. Drizzle artichokes with lemon juice. Place upside down in steamer
basket over boiling water in large saucepan. Cover. Steam for about
30 minutes until base is tender and inner leaf can be pulled away easily.
Set upside down on paper towels or wire rack for 5 minutes to drain. Cut
in half. Scoop out and discard centre. Quarter artichokes. Remove and
discard any tough outer leaves.

Cook bacon in large frying pan on medium for 5 to 8 minutes until crisp.
Remove to paper towel to drain. Reserve 1 tbsp. (15 mL) drippings.

Heat reserved drippings in same frying pan on medium-low. Add onion and
garlic. Cook for about 10 minutes, stirring occasionally, until onion is soft.

Add wine, tomatoes and pepper. Stir. Bring to a boil on medium-high. Boil
for about 5 minutes until thickened. Add bacon and artichoke. Stir. Cook
for 3 to 5 minutes until heated through.

Add basil. Stir. Makes 2 1/2 cups (625 mL).

1/2 cup (125 mL): 150 Calories; 5.4 g Total Fat (2.5 g Mono, 0.8 g Poly, 1.8 g Sat);
9 mg Cholesterol; 19 g Carbohydrate; 5 g Fibre; 8 g Protein; 390 mg Sodium

Rapini And Browned Garlic

Also known as "broccoli raab," rapini has a pungent, earthy flavour
that goes very well with the browned garlic and teriyaki sauce in this dish.
Serve with grilled fish or pork.

Hard margarine (or butter)	2 tbsp.	30 mL
Elephant (or very large) garlic cloves, peeled and chopped	4	4
Hard margarine (or butter)	1 tbsp.	15 mL
Thick teriyaki sauce	1/2 cup	125 mL
Brown sugar, packed	2 tsp.	10 mL
Rapini (or broccoli raab), about 2 bunches, trimmed of tough ends	2 lbs.	900 g
Water		

Melt first amount of margarine in frying pan on medium-low. Add garlic. Cook for about 15 minutes, stirring occasionally, until soft and golden. Transfer garlic to small bowl. Cool.

Melt second amount of margarine in same frying pan. Add teriyaki sauce and brown sugar. Heat and stir for 1 to 2 minutes until bubbling and brown sugar is dissolved. Remove from heat, but keep warm.

Coarsely chop rapini crosswise 3 or 4 times. Cook in water in large pot or Dutch oven for about 2 minutes until bright green and barely tender. Do not overcook. Drain well. Arrange on platter or put into large bowl. Drizzle with sauce. Sprinkle with garlic. Makes 6 cups (1.5 L).

1/2 cup (125 mL): 62 Calories; 3.2 g Total Fat (0.9 g Mono, 0.2 g Poly, 1.9 g Sat); 8 mg Cholesterol; 7 g Carbohydrate; 2 g Fibre; 3 g Protein; 537 mg Sodium

Paré Pointer

He thought his math book almost had tears on it.
It had so many problems.

Belgian Endive Bake

This recipe takes a little extra time to prepare, but it's so worth the effort! The delicious, creamy texture would be the perfect accompaniment to roasted pork, chicken or beef.

Stalks of Belgian endive	6	6
Hard margarine (or butter)	1 tbsp.	15 mL
Granulated sugar	1 tbsp.	15 mL
Salt	1/2 tsp.	2 mL
Pepper	1/4 tsp.	1 mL
Bacon slices, diced	4	4
All-purpose flour	2 tbsp.	30 mL
Half-and-half cream	1 2/3 cups	400 mL
Finely grated fresh Parmesan cheese	1/4 cup	60 mL
Fine dry bread crumbs	1/3 cup	75 mL

Place endive in greased shallow 1 1/2 quart (1.5 L) casserole. Dot with margarine. Sprinkle with sugar, salt and pepper. Cover. Cook in 350°F (175°C) oven for about 1 1/2 hours until soft. Drain and discard any liquid. Set aside.

Cook bacon in medium saucepan on medium for about 5 minutes until crisp. Remove to paper towel to drain. Reserve 1 tbsp. (15 mL) drippings.

Heat reserved drippings in same pan on medium. Add flour. Heat and stir until bubbling. Gradually stir in cream. Heat and stir for about 5 minutes until boiling and thickened. Pour over endive.

Sprinkle with bacon, cheese and bread crumbs. Bake, uncovered, in 350°F (175°C) oven for about 15 minutes until bubbling and lightly browned. Makes about 4 cups (1 L).

1/2 cup (125 mL): 148 Calories; 9.7 g Total Fat (3.6 g Mono, 0.7 g Poly, 4.9 g Sat); 22 mg Cholesterol; 11 g Carbohydrate; trace Fibre; 5 g Protein; 341 mg Sodium

Garlic Potato And Swiss Chard

This is a delicious way to add greens to your potatoes.
You'll love the comforting garlic flavour and the creamy texture.

Medium potatoes (about 2 lbs., 900 g), peeled and quartered	4	4
Water		
Salt	1/2 tsp.	2 mL
Hard margarine (or butter)	2 tbsp.	30 mL
Finely chopped red onion	1/2 cup	125 mL
Garlic cloves, minced (or 1/2 tsp., 2 mL, powder)	2	2
Salt	1/4 tsp.	1 mL
Anchovy paste	1/2 tsp.	2 mL
Whipping cream (or milk)	3 tbsp.	50 mL
Bunch of Swiss chard, stems removed and leaves chopped (about 5 cups, 1.25 L)	1	1

Cook potato in water and first amount of salt in large saucepan for about 20 minutes until soft. Drain. Mash until no lumps remain.

Melt margarine in large frying pan on medium-low. Add onion, garlic and second amount of salt. Cook for about 10 minutes, stirring occasionally, until onion is soft.

Add anchovy paste and whipping cream. Stir.

Add Swiss chard. Heat and stir on medium for 3 to 5 minutes until chard is wilted. Add to potato. Mix well. Makes about 4 cups (1 L).

1/2 cup (125 mL): 133 Calories; 4.9 g Total Fat (2.4 g Mono, 0.4 g Poly, 1.8 g Sat); 7 mg Cholesterol; 20 g Carbohydrate; 2 g Fibre; 3 g Protein; 183 mg Sodium

 If you cook with garlic often, prepare larger amounts in advance. Simply chop several cloves and put into a small amount of olive oil in a jar with a tight-fitting lid. Store in refrigerator for up to 2 weeks.

Green Tomato Chutney

A chunky, sweet and spicy chutney that can be
made ahead of time for unexpected company.

Green tomatoes, chopped	3 lbs.	1.4 kg
Chopped onion	1 cup	250 mL
Brown sugar, packed	2 cups	500 mL
Apple cider vinegar	1 1/2 cups	375 mL
Dark raisins	3/4 cup	175 mL
Ground ginger	1 tsp.	5 mL
Ground coriander	1 tsp.	5 mL
Cayenne pepper	1 tsp.	5 mL
Salt	1 tsp.	5 mL

Combine all 9 ingredients in large pot or Dutch oven. Bring to a boil. Boil gently, uncovered, on medium for about 1 hour until thickened. Fill hot sterilized jars to within 1/2 inch (12 mm) of top. Place sterilized metal lids on jars and screw metal bands on securely. Process in boiling water bath for 15 minutes. Makes 6 half pint (1 cup, 250 mL) jars.

1 tbsp. (15 mL): 26 Calories; trace Total Fat (trace Mono, trace Poly, trace Sat); 0 mg Cholesterol;
7 g Carbohydrate; trace Fibre; trace Protein; 28 mg Sodium

Pictured on page 126.

1. Spinach Squash Salad, page 48
2. Fruity Butter Lettuce Salad, page 75
3. Orange Butter Beans, page 135

Props Courtesy Of: Linens 'N Things
The Bay
Winners Stores

Sesame Snow Peas

Toasted sesame seeds add visual interest to this beautiful, bright green dish.
This tastes great with marinated chicken and grilled fish.

Cooking oil	2 tsp.	10 mL
Chopped green onion	1/2 cup	125 mL
Rice vinegar	1 tbsp.	15 mL
Granulated sugar	2 tsp.	10 mL
Sesame oil	1 tsp.	5 mL
Fresh snow pea pods, trimmed	3/4 lb.	340 g
Sesame seeds, toasted (see Tip, page 86)	2 tbsp.	30 mL
Lemon juice	1 tbsp.	15 mL

Heat cooking oil in large frying pan on medium-high. Add next
4 ingredients. Heat and stir for about 1 minute until sugar is dissolved.

Add pea pods. Cook for about 3 minutes, stirring often, until tender-crisp.

Add sesame seeds and lemon juice. Stir. Makes about 3 cups (750 mL).

1/2 cup (125 mL): 80 Calories; 5.1 g Total Fat (2.4 g Mono, 1.9 g Poly, 0.6 g Sat); 0 mg Cholesterol;
7 g Carbohydrate; 2 g Fibre; 2 g Protein; 5 mg Sodium

1. Devilled Peas, page 118
2. Minted Pea Salad, page 98
3. Lettuce Wedges Salad, page 20
4. Green Tomato Chutney, page 124

Props Courtesy Of: Anchor Hocking Canada
Bernardin Ltd.
Canhome Global

Broccoli In Blue Cheese Sauce

Crisp, green broccoli florets are drizzled with a thick, warm sauce.
If you're a fan of blue cheese, you'll delight in this creamy combination.

BLUE CHEESE SAUCE

Cooking oil	1 tbsp.	15 mL
Finely chopped onion	1/3 cup	75 mL
Garlic clove, minced (or 1/4 tsp., 1 mL, powder)	1	1
All-purpose flour	1 tbsp.	15 mL
Milk	1 1/2 cups	375 mL
Crumbled blue cheese (about 1 oz., 28 g)	3 tbsp.	50 mL
Chopped fresh chives (or 1 1/2 tsp., 7 mL, dried)	2 tbsp.	30 mL
Salt	1/2 tsp.	2 mL
Pepper	1/8 tsp.	0.5 mL
Broccoli florets	5 cups	1.25 L
Water		
Salt	1/4 tsp.	1 mL

Blue Cheese Sauce: Heat cooking oil in medium saucepan on medium. Add onion and garlic. Cook for about 5 minutes, stirring occasionally, until onion is soft.

Add flour. Heat and stir for 1 minute. Gradually stir in milk. Heat and stir for about 10 minutes until boiling and thickened. Remove from heat.

Add next 4 ingredients. Stir until well combined. Makes about 1 1/4 cups (300 mL) sauce.

Cook broccoli in water and salt in large saucepan until tender-crisp. Drain well. Drizzle sauce over top. Stir. Makes about 5 cups (1.25 L).

1/2 cup (125 mL): 56 Calories; 2.7 g Total Fat (1.2 g Mono, 0.5 g Poly, 0.9 g Sat); 3 mg Cholesterol; 6 g Carbohydrate; 1 g Fibre; 3 g Protein; 187 mg Sodium

Zucchini Cheese Rolls

Lightly grilled zucchini rolls stuffed with a scrumptious cheese and fresh herb filling. Cut these delicious morsels in half before serving to reveal an attractive cheese spiral.

Ingredient	Imperial	Metric
Soft goat (chèvre) cheese	3 1/2 oz.	100 g
Block of cream cheese, softened	4 oz.	125 g
Chopped sun-dried tomatoes in oil, drained	3 tbsp.	50 mL
Chopped fresh parsley (or 1 1/2 tsp., 7 mL, flakes)	2 tbsp.	30 mL
Chopped fresh chives (or 1 1/2 tsp., 7 mL, dried)	2 tbsp.	30 mL
Coarsely ground pepper (or 1/4 tsp., 1 mL, pepper)	1/2 tsp.	2 mL
Medium zucchini (with peel), cut lengthwise into 1/4 inch (6 mm) slices	2	2
Olive (or cooking) oil	2 tbsp.	30 mL
Salt, sprinkle		

Put first 6 ingredients into small bowl. Mash with fork. Let stand at room temperature.

Brush both sides of each zucchini slice with olive oil. Sprinkle with salt. Preheat electric grill for 5 minutes or gas barbecue to medium. Cook zucchini on greased grill for 3 to 5 minutes per side until tender-crisp and grill marks appear. Spread each zucchini slice with 1 1/2 to 2 tbsp. (25 to 30 mL) cheese mixture. Roll up to enclose mixture. Serve cold or at room temperature. Makes 10 to 12 rolls.

1 roll: 114 Calories; 10.4 g Total Fat (4.1 g Mono, 0.5 g Poly, 5.2 g Sat); 22 mg Cholesterol; 2 g Carbohydrate; 1 g Fibre; 4 g Protein; 96 mg Sodium

Pictured on page 143.

 Most of us slice tomatoes crosswise. To retain more juice—and to make less mess on your countertop—try slicing tomatoes vertically.

Butter Pecan Peas

These sweet green pea pods are coated in warm,
savoury butter and cooked to perfection.

Butter (or hard margarine)	2 tbsp.	30 mL
Garlic clove, minced (or 1/4 tsp., 1 mL, powder)	1	1
Sugar snap pea pods (about 1 lb., 454 g), trimmed	4 cups	1 L
Pecans, toasted (see Tip, page 86) and coarsely chopped	1/3 cup	75 mL
Brown sugar, packed	1 tbsp.	15 mL
Lemon juice	1 tbsp.	15 mL
Coarsely ground pepper (or 1/4 tsp., 1 mL, pepper)	1/2 tsp.	2 mL

Melt butter in large saucepan on medium. Add garlic. Heat and stir for about 1 minute until fragrant.

Add remaining 5 ingredients. Cook for about 6 minutes, stirring often, until pea pods are tender-crisp. Makes about 4 cups (1 L).

1/2 cup (125 mL): 90 Calories; 6.5 g Total Fat (3 g Mono, 1 g Poly, 2.1 g Sat); 8 mg Cholesterol; 7 g Carbohydrate; 1 g Fibre; 2 g Protein; 33 mg Sodium

Herbed Brussels Sprouts

The secret to good Brussels sprouts is not to overcook them.
Toss them with butter and fresh herbs to really bring out their flavour.

Chopped fresh mint leaves (or 3/4 – 1 1/2 tsp., 4 – 7 mL, dried)	1 – 2 tbsp.	15 – 30 mL
Chopped fresh sweet basil (or 3/4 – 1 1/2 tsp., 4 – 7 mL, dried)	1 – 2 tbsp.	15 – 30 mL
Olive (or cooking) oil	2 tbsp.	30 mL
Hard margarine (or butter), melted	2 tbsp.	30 mL
Lemon juice	2 tbsp.	30 mL
Grainy mustard	2 tsp.	10 mL
Salt	1/4 tsp.	1 mL
Pepper	1/4 tsp.	1 mL

(continued on next page)

| Brussels sprouts, trimmed of tough outer leaves | 2 lbs. | 900 g |
| Water | | |

Process first 8 ingredients in blender until smooth.

Cook Brussels sprouts in water in large saucepan for 6 to 8 minutes until tender-crisp. Drain. Add herb mixture. Heat and stir for 1 to 2 minutes until hot. Makes about 5 cups (1.25 L).

1/2 cup (125 mL): 79 Calories; 5.6 g Total Fat (3.6 g Mono, 0.7 g Poly, 1 g Sat); 0 mg Cholesterol; 8 g Carbohydrate; 3 g Fibre; 2 g Protein; 120 mg Sodium

---

Sesame Bok Choy

These soft greens are coated in a dark hoisin sauce with an intense sesame aftertaste. This side dish would go well with steamed rice and grilled pork or chicken.

Cooking oil	2 tsp.	10 mL
Bunch of Shanghai bok choy (about 2 lbs., 900 g), trimmed and separated	1	1
Cornstarch	1 tsp.	5 mL
Water	1 tbsp.	15 mL
Rice vinegar	1 tbsp.	15 mL
Hoisin sauce	1 tbsp.	15 mL
Soy sauce	2 tsp.	10 mL
Sesame oil	1 tsp.	5 mL
Sesame seeds, toasted (see Tip, page 86)	2 tbsp.	30 mL

Heat cooking oil in wok or large frying pan on medium-high. Add bok choy. Stir-fry for 1 minute.

Combine next 6 ingredients in small cup. Add to bok choy. Stir-fry for 3 to 5 minutes until bok choy stems are tender-crisp and leaves are wilted.

Sprinkle with sesame seeds. Makes about 3 cups (750 mL).

1/2 cup (125 mL): 66 Calories; 4.1 g Total Fat (1.8 g Mono, 1.6 g Poly, 0.5 g Sat); 0 mg Cholesterol; 6 g Carbohydrate; 2 g Fibre; 3 g Protein; 273 mg Sodium

Porcini-Sauced Fiddleheads

Fresh, earthy-tasting fiddleheads are such a special treat when they're well prepared. For the best results, you should make the creamy mushroom sauce first and then just barely cook the fiddleheads before serving.

PORCINI BUTTER SAUCE

Boiling water	2/3 cup	150 mL
Dried porcini mushrooms (about 1/4 oz., 7 g)	1/4 cup	60 mL
Butter (or hard margarine)	2 tbsp.	30 mL
Garlic clove, cut in half	1	1
Finely chopped shallots (or green onion)	1 tbsp.	15 mL
Salt, sprinkle		
Coarsely ground pepper, sprinkle		
All-purpose flour	2 tsp.	10 mL
Dry sherry	2 tsp.	10 mL
Whipping cream (or milk)	2 tbsp.	30 mL
Finely chopped fresh parsley (or 1/4 tsp., 1 mL, flakes)	1 tsp.	5 mL
Fresh (or frozen, thawed) fiddleheads	10 oz.	285 g
Water		

Porcini Butter Sauce: Pour boiling water over mushrooms in small dish. Let stand for 15 minutes until soft. Remove mushrooms, reserving liquid. Dice finely. Set aside. Strain reserved liquid through very fine sieve or 2 layers of cheesecloth. Discard solids.

Melt butter in small saucepan on medium. Add garlic and shallots. Sprinkle with salt and pepper. Cook for about 2 minutes, stirring often, until shallots are soft. Remove and discard garlic.

Add flour to butter mixture. Heat and stir until combined. Add reserved mushroom liquid, mushrooms and sherry. Heat and stir until boiling and slightly thickened.

Stir in whipping cream and parsley. Heat through. Keep warm. Makes 3/4 cup (175 mL) sauce.

(continued on next page)

Cook fiddleheads in water in large saucepan for 1 to 2 minutes unt
green and tender-crisp. Drain. Turn into serving bowl. Drizzle with
Makes about 3 cups (750 mL).

1/2 cup (125 mL): 69 Calories; 5.7 g Total Fat (3 g Mono, 0.4 g Poly, 1.8 g Sat); 6 mg Cholesterol; 4 g Carbohydrate; 1 g Fibre; 2 g Protein; 48 mg Sodium

---

Pepper Mango Salsa

Use fresh mangoes in this vibrant, chunky salsa when they're in season. Serve with grilled chicken or salmon for a special treat.

Garlic clove, minced (or 1/4 tsp., 1 mL, powder)	1	1
Lime juice	1 tbsp.	15 mL
Peanut (or cooking) oil	1 tbsp.	15 mL
Sweet (or regular) chili sauce	1 tbsp.	15 mL
Salt	1/4 tsp.	1 mL
Finely chopped green pepper	1 cup	250 mL
Can of sliced mangoes, drained and chopped	14 oz.	398 mL
Chopped green onion	1/4 cup	60 mL
Chopped fresh cilantro (or fresh parsley)	2 tbsp.	30 mL

Combine first 5 ingredients in medium bowl.

Add remaining 4 ingredients. Toss until coated. Makes about 2 1/2 cups (625 mL).

1/2 cup (125 mL): 68 Calories; 3 g Total Fat (1.3 g Mono, 0.9 g Poly, 0.5 g Sat); 0 mg Cholesterol; 11 g Carbohydrate; 2 g Fibre; 1 g Protein; 168 mg Sodium

Pictured on page 17.

Beans In Mushroom Sauce

Fresh mushrooms and crisp green beans taste
absolutely delicious in this inviting, cheesy sauce.

MUSHROOM SAUCE

Cooking oil	1 tbsp.	15 mL
Fresh white mushrooms, sliced	1 1/2 cups	375 mL
Garlic clove, minced (or 1/4 tsp., 1 mL, powder)	1	1
Dry white (or alcohol-free) wine	1/4 cup	60 mL
Whipping cream (or milk)	2/3 cup	150 mL
Salt	1/4 tsp.	1 mL
Fresh green beans, cut into 2 inch (5 cm) pieces	1 lb.	454 g
Water		
Finely grated fresh Parmesan cheese	3 tbsp.	50 mL

Mushroom Sauce: Heat cooking oil in medium frying pan on medium-high. Add mushrooms and garlic. Cook for 5 to 7 minutes, stirring occasionally, until mushrooms are lightly browned.

Add wine. Cook for about 30 seconds until almost all liquid is evaporated.

Add whipping cream and salt. Heat and stir for 1 to 3 minutes until thickened.

Cook beans in water in large saucepan for about 5 minutes until tender-crisp. Drain. Add mushroom mixture. Stir.

Sprinkle with cheese. Makes about 3 cups (750 mL).

1/2 cup (125 mL): 154 Calories; 12.4 g Total Fat (4.3 g Mono, 1.1 g Poly, 6.4 g Sat);
35 mg Cholesterol; 7 g Carbohydrate; 2 g Fibre; 4 g Protein; 174 mg Sodium

Orange Butter Beans

Bright green beans, accented with red pepper and red onion,
are coated in a sweet, orange-flavoured, buttery sauce.

ORANGE BUTTER

Butter (or hard margarine)	2 tbsp.	30 mL
Finely chopped red onion	1/3 cup	75 mL
Garlic clove, minced (or 1/4 tsp., 1 mL, powder)	1	1
Finely chopped red pepper	1/3 cup	75 mL
Orange juice	3 tbsp.	50 mL
Liquid honey	2 tbsp.	30 mL
Salt	1/4 tsp.	1 mL
Pepper, just a pinch		
Fresh green beans	1 lb.	454 g
Water	1 cup	250 mL

Orange Butter: Melt butter in large frying pan on medium-low. Add next 3 ingredients. Cook for about 10 minutes, stirring occasionally, until onion and r̶e̶d̶ ̶p̶e̶p̶p̶e̶r̶ ̶a̶r̶e̶ soft.

̶A̶d̶d̶ ̶n̶e̶x̶t̶ ̶2̶ ingredients. Stir. Simmer for 2 to 3 minutes.

̶C̶o̶o̶k̶ ̶b̶e̶a̶n̶s̶ ̶i̶n̶ ̶w̶a̶t̶er in large saucepan for 5 to 6 minutes until ̶t̶e̶n̶d̶e̶r̶-̶c̶r̶i̶s̶p̶.̶ Add to orange juice mixture. Toss until coated. ̶M̶a̶k̶e̶s̶ ̶3̶ ̶c̶u̶p̶s̶ (750 mL).

̶1̶/̶2̶ ̶c̶u̶p̶ ̶(̶1̶2̶5̶ ̶m̶L̶)̶:̶ ̶7̶4̶ ̶C̶a̶lories; 4 g Total Fat (1.1 g Mono, 0.2 g Poly, 2.5 g Sat); 11 mg Cholesterol;
̶1̶ ̶g̶ ̶F̶i̶bre; 2 g Protein; 144 mg Sodium

̶P̶i̶c̶t̶u̶r̶e̶d̶ ̶o̶n̶ ̶p̶a̶g̶e̶ 25 and on back cover.

Paré Pointer

̶C̶r̶o̶s̶s̶ ̶a̶ ̶v̶ampire with Al Capone and you have a fangster.

Gazpacho

You'll love the fresh dill in this deep red, easy-to-make cold soup.
Serve with a dollop of sour cream for an attractive finish.

Medium tomatoes, peeled and coarsely chopped	6	6
English cucumber (with peel), coarsely chopped	1	1
Coarsely chopped red onion	3/4 cup	175 mL
Garlic cloves, minced (or 1/2 tsp., 2 mL, powder)	2	2
Chopped fresh dill (or 1 1/2 tsp., 7 mL, dill weed)	2 tbsp.	30 mL
Balsamic vinegar	2 tbsp.	30 mL
Granulated sugar	1 tsp.	5 mL
Hot pepper sauce	1 tsp.	5 mL
Salt	1/2 tsp.	2 mL
Coarsely ground pepper (or 1/8 tsp., 0.5 mL, pepper)	1/4 tsp.	1 mL
Can of tomato juice	19 oz.	540 mL
Large avocado, finely chopped	1	1

Put first 10 ingredients into food processor. Pulse with on/off motion for about 20 seconds until chopped. Put into large bowl.

Add tomato juice. Stir. Cover. Chill for at least 3 hours or overnight.

Scatter avocado over individual servings. Makes about 7 1/2 cups (1.9 L).

1 cup (250 mL): 93 Calories; 4.6 g Total Fat (2.6 g Mono, 0.7 g Poly, 0.7 g Sat); 0 mg Cholesterol; 14 g Carbohydrate; 3 g Fibre; 3 g Protein; 440 mg Sodium

tip   *Adding greens to soups towards the end of cooking is a great way to create unique flavours and colours. For a touch of spice, add arugula or mustard greens; for a cabbage flavour, use kale; for a delicate beet flavour, use beet greens or Swiss chard.*

Parsley Butter Soup

A smooth, golden soup mixed with a rich butter flavour and fresh parsley.

Butter (or hard margarine)	1/4 cup	60 mL
Chopped onion	1 1/2 cups	375 mL
Chopped carrot	1 1/2 cups	375 mL
Garlic cloves, minced (or 3/4 tsp., 4 mL, powder)	3	3
Prepared chicken broth	4 cups	1 L
Chopped potato	3 cups	750 mL
Chopped fresh parsley	1 cup	250 mL
Salt	1/4 tsp.	1 mL
Pepper, just a pinch		
Chopped fresh parsley, for garnish		

Melt butter in large pot or Dutch oven on medium-low. Add onion, carrot and garlic. Cook for about 10 minutes, stirring occasionally, until onion is soft.

Add broth and potato. Stir. Bring to a boil. Reduce heat to medium-low. Cover. Simmer for about 30 minutes until potato is tender.

Add first amount of parsley, salt and pepper. Stir. Cool slightly. Process in blender until smooth. Return to pot. Heat and stir on medium for 2 to 3 minutes until mixture is hot.

Garnish individual servings with second amount of parsley. Makes about 7 cups (1.75 L).

1 cup (250 mL): 169 Calories; 8.1 g Total Fat (2.4 g Mono, 0.5 g Poly, 4.6 g Sat); 19 mg Cholesterol; 19 g Carbohydrate; 2 g Fibre; 5 g Protein; 644 mg Sodium

Paré Pointer

If your diet calls for only one slice of bread, simply slice the loaf lengthwise.

Creamy Asparagus Soup

This delicious soup will become a favourite! The smooth,
creamy texture will keep your guests coming back for more.

Cooking oil	1 tbsp.	15 mL
Hard margarine (or butter)	1 tbsp.	15 mL
Chopped leek (white and tender parts only)	1 1/2 cups	375 mL
Garlic cloves, minced (or 1/2 tsp., 2 mL, powder)	2	2
All-purpose flour	1 tbsp.	15 mL
Dry white (or alcohol-free) wine	1/4 cup	60 mL
Prepared chicken broth	4 cups	1 L
Chopped potato	1 1/2 cups	375 mL
Asparagus, trimmed of tough ends and chopped (tips reserved)	2 lbs.	900 g
Salt	1/4 tsp.	1 mL
Whipping cream	1 cup	250 mL

Chopped fresh parsley, for garnish
Coarsely ground pepper, sprinkle

Heat cooking oil and margarine in large pot or Dutch oven on medium-low. Add leek and garlic. Cook for about 10 minutes, stirring occasionally, until leek is tender.

Add flour. Heat and stir for about 1 minute until smooth.

Add wine. Heat and stir until thickened.

Add broth and potato. Bring to a boil. Reduce heat to medium. Simmer, uncovered, for about 10 minutes until potato is just tender.

Add asparagus (not tips) and salt. Cook for 5 to 7 minutes until asparagus is tender. Cool slightly. Process in blender, in 2 batches, until smooth. Return to pot.

Add reserved asparagus tips and whipping cream. Heat and stir on medium-high for about 5 minutes until asparagus tips are tender-crisp and mixture is heated through.

(continued on next page)

Sprinkle individual servings with parsley and pepper. Makes about 10 cups (2.5 L).

1 cup (250 mL): 171 Calories; 11.5 g Total Fat (4.2 g Mono, 1 g Poly, 5.6 g Sat); 29 mg Cholesterol; 12 g Carbohydrate; 2 g Fibre; 5 g Protein; 417 mg Sodium

Pictured on page 144.

Green Pepper And Ham Soup

A very pretty, orange soup with a sensational smoky aftertaste.

Olive (or cooking) oil	1 tbsp.	15 mL
Chopped green pepper	2 cups	500 mL
Chopped leek (white and tender parts only)	1 1/2 cups	375 mL
Chopped celery	1/2 cup	125 mL
Garlic cloves, minced (or 1 tsp., 5 mL, powder)	4	4
Chili paste (sambal oelek)	1 tsp.	5 mL
Smoked ham bones	1 1/2 lbs.	680 g
Medium tomatoes, peeled and chopped	6	6
Prepared chicken broth	3 cups	750 mL
Water	3 cups	750 mL
Chopped carrot	1 1/2 cups	375 mL
Can of white kidney beans, rinsed and drained	19 oz.	540 mL
Chopped fresh mint leaves (or 2 1/4 tsp., 11 mL, dried)	3 tbsp.	50 mL

Heat olive oil in large pot or Dutch oven on medium. Add next 5 ingredients. Stir. Cook for about 10 minutes, stirring occasionally, until leek is tender.

Add next 5 ingredients. Bring to a boil. Cover. Simmer on low for about 2 hours until ham is tender. Remove ham bones. Chop meat. Discard bones. Return meat to pot. Chill overnight. Remove and discard fat from top.

Add beans and mint. Heat on medium for 10 to 15 minutes, stirring occasionally, until hot. Makes about 14 cups (3.5 L).

1 cup (250 mL): 107 Calories; 3.5 g Total Fat (1.7 g Mono, 0.5 g Poly, 0.9 g Sat); 11 mg Cholesterol; 12 g Carbohydrate; 2 g Fibre; 8 g Protein; 505 mg Sodium

Simple Greens Soup

A classic vegetable soup recipe that includes heaps of healthy ingredients.
A warm, delicious dish to come home to.

Leeks (white and tender parts only), thinly sliced (about 3 cups, 750 mL)	3	3
Medium zucchini (with peel), about 1 1/2 lbs. (680 g), diced	3	3
Chopped celery	1 cup	250 mL
All-purpose flour	3 tbsp.	50 mL
Prepared vegetable (or chicken) broth	4 cups	1 L
Can of stewed tomatoes (with juice), processed in blender until smooth	14 oz.	398 mL
Salt	1 tsp.	5 mL
Pepper, sprinkle		
Coarsely chopped spinach, stems removed, lightly packed	3 cups	750 mL
Chopped fresh parsley (or dill), not dried	2 tbsp.	30 mL
Balsamic vinegar	2 tbsp.	30 mL
Diced seeded tomato, for garnish	3/4 cup	175 mL
Grated fresh Parmesan (or Romano) cheese, for garnish	1/2 cup	125 mL
Chopped fresh parsley (or dill), for garnish	2 tbsp.	30 mL

Put first 4 ingredients into 4 to 5 quart (4 to 5 L) slow cooker. Stir.

Stir in broth, tomatoes, salt and pepper. Cover. Cook on Low for 7 to 8 hours or on High for 3 1/2 to 4 hours until vegetables are very tender.

Add spinach, first amount of parsley and vinegar. Stir. Cover. Cook on High for about 10 minutes until spinach is wilted.

Garnish individual servings with tomato, cheese and second amount of parsley. Makes 11 cups (2.75 L).

1 cup (250 mL): 90 Calories; 2.3 g Total Fat (0.7 g Mono, 0.3 g Poly, 1.1 g Sat); 4 mg Cholesterol; 13 g Carbohydrate; 3 g Fibre; 6 g Protein; 735 mg Sodium

Zucchini And Fennel Soup

A chunky, rich-looking broth that is brimming with tender-crisp vegetables.
Increase the amount of chili paste if you prefer a bit more spice.

Bacon slices, diced	6	6
Chopped red onion	1 cup	250 mL
Garlic cloves, minced (or 1/2 tsp., 2 mL, powder)	2	2
Chili paste (sambal oelek)	1 tsp.	5 mL
Prepared chicken broth	4 cups	1 L
Large tomatoes, peeled and chopped	4	4
Fennel bulb (white part only), thinly sliced	1	1
Tomato paste	1/4 cup	60 mL
Granulated sugar	2 tsp.	10 mL
Chopped zucchini (with peel)	2 cups	500 mL
Salt	1/2 tsp.	2 mL
Pepper	1/4 tsp.	1 mL
Chopped fresh dill (or 3/4 – 1 1/2 tsp., 4 – 7 mL, dill weed)	1 – 2 tbsp.	15 – 30 mL

Cook bacon in large pot or Dutch oven on medium for about 10 minutes until crisp. Remove to paper towels to drain. Reserve 1 tbsp. (15 mL) drippings.

Heat reserved drippings in same pot on medium-low. Add onion, garlic and chili paste. Cook for about 10 minutes, stirring occasionally, until onion is soft.

Add next 5 ingredients. Stir. Cook, uncovered, for about 30 minutes, stirring occasionally, until fennel is tender.

Add bacon, zucchini, salt and pepper. Stir. Cook for about 5 minutes, stirring occasionally, until zucchini is tender.

Add dill. Stir. Makes about 9 cups (2.25 L).

1 cup (250 mL): 87 Calories; 3.2 g Total Fat (1.3 g Mono, 0.5 g Poly, 1 g Sat); 4 mg Cholesterol; 11 g Carbohydrate; 2 g Fibre; 5 g Protein; 590 mg Sodium

Curried Sweet Potato Soup

The perfect soup to serve on a cold winter day.

Cooking oil	1 tbsp.	15 mL
Chopped onion	1 cup	250 mL
Mild curry paste	2 tbsp.	30 mL
Prepared chicken broth	4 cups	1 L
Chopped sweet potato (or yam)	4 cups	1 L
Salt	1/2 tsp.	2 mL
Pepper	1/2 tsp.	2 mL
Fresh (or frozen) peas	3 cups	750 mL
Coconut milk	1 cup	250 mL

Ribbon (or fancy flake) coconut, for garnish
Chopped fresh parsley, for garnish

Heat cooking oil in large pot or Dutch oven on medium-low. Add onion and curry paste. Cook for about 10 minutes, stirring occasionally, until onion is soft.

Add next 4 ingredients. Stir. Bring to a boil. Reduce heat to medium. Cook, uncovered, for 15 to 20 minutes until sweet potato is tender.

Add peas. Stir. Cook for 5 to 7 minutes until tender. Cool slightly. Process in blender, in batches, until smooth. Return to pot.

Add coconut milk. Heat and stir on medium for about 5 minutes until very hot, but not boiling.

Sprinkle individual servings with coconut and parsley. Makes about 7 1/2 cups (1.9 L).

1 cup (250 mL): 253 Calories; 11.3 g Total Fat (2.5 g Mono, 1.4 g Poly, 6.6 g Sat); 0 mg Cholesterol; 31 g Carbohydrate; 3 g Fibre; 8 g Protein; 614 mg Sodium

Pictured on page 144.

1. Spinach Pasta Salad, page 40
2. Zucchini Cheese Rolls, page 129
3. Zucchini Clusters, page 113

Props Courtesy Of: Canhome Global
Pier 1 Imports

Cream Of Celery Soup

*A delicately seasoned soup that is smooth and creamy
without being too rich. This is truly delicious!*

Hard margarine (or butter)	3 tbsp.	50 mL
Chopped celery (ribs and leaves)	2 cups	500 mL
Chopped green onion	1 cup	250 mL
All-purpose flour	2 tbsp.	30 mL
Prepared chicken (or vegetable) broth	2 cups	500 mL
Milk	2 cups	500 mL
Chopped potato	1 1/2 cups	375 mL
Salt	1/2 tsp.	2 mL
Pepper	1/8 tsp.	0.5 mL

Melt margarine in large pot or Dutch oven on medium-low. Add celery
and green onion. Cook for about 15 minutes, stirring occasionally, until
celery is tender.

Add flour. Heat and stir for about 1 minute until smooth. Gradually stir
in broth.

Add remaining 4 ingredients. Stir. Bring to a boil. Reduce heat to
medium-low. Cook, uncovered, for about 15 minutes, stirring occasionally,
until potato is tender. Cool slightly. Process in blender, in 2 batches, until
smooth. Return to pot. Heat and stir on medium for about 5 minutes until
heated through. Makes about 6 cups (1.5 L).

*1 cup (250 mL): 155 Calories; 7.4 g Total Fat (4.3 g Mono, 0.8 g Poly, 1.9 g Sat); 3 mg Cholesterol;
17 g Carbohydrate; 2 g Fibre; 6 g Protein; 624 mg Sodium*

1. Creamy Asparagus Soup, page 138
2. Curried Sweet Potato Soup, page 142
3. Minestrone And Pesto, page 146

Soups

Minestrone And Pesto

This delicious soup takes a little extra time to prepare, but it is well worth it!

Italian sausages, casings removed	4	4
Olive (or cooking) oil	1 tbsp.	15 mL
Chopped leek (white and tender parts only)	1 cup	250 mL
Chopped green pepper	1 cup	250 mL
Chopped celery	1/2 cup	125 mL
Garlic cloves, minced (or 1/2 tsp., 2 mL, powder)	2	2
Medium tomatoes, peeled and chopped	6	6
Prepared chicken broth	6 cups	1.5 L
Very small pasta (such as bow, alpha or orzo)	1/2 cup	125 mL
Granulated sugar	1 tsp.	5 mL
Salt	1/4 tsp.	1 mL
Coarsely ground pepper (or 1/8 tsp., 0.5 mL, pepper)	1/4 tsp.	1 mL
Spinach, stems removed, coarsely chopped	2 cups	500 mL
Chopped fresh green beans	1 1/2 cups	375 mL
Fresh (or frozen) peas	1 cup	250 mL
PESTO		
Fresh sweet basil (not dried), packed	1/2 cup	125 mL
Pecans, toasted (see Tip, page 86)	1/4 cup	60 mL
Finely grated fresh Parmesan cheese	1/4 cup	60 mL
Garlic clove (or 1/4 tsp., 1 mL, powder)	1	1
Balsamic vinegar	2 tsp.	10 mL
Olive (or cooking) oil	3 tbsp.	50 mL

Grated fresh Parmesan cheese, for garnish

Cook sausages in medium frying pan on medium for 15 to 20 minutes, turning occasionally, until completely cooked. Chop into 1/3 inch (1 cm) pieces. Set aside.

Heat olive oil in large pot or Dutch oven on medium-low. Add next 4 ingredients. Cook for about 10 minutes, stirring occasionally, until leek is tender.

Add sausage and next 6 ingredients. Bring to a boil. Reduce heat to medium-low. Simmer, uncovered, for 20 minutes, stirring occasionally.

(continued on next page)

Soups

Add spinach, beans and peas. Heat and stir for 5 to 7 minutes until beans are tender. Makes about 12 cups (3 L).

Pesto: Process first 5 ingredients in food processor until smooth.

With motor running, add olive oil through feed chute in thin steady stream until well combined. Makes about 1/2 cup (125 mL) pesto. Add about 1 tbsp. (15 mL) to individual servings. Stir.

Sprinkle individual servings with cheese.

1 cup (250 mL): 242 Calories; 14 g Total Fat (7.7 g Mono, 1.9 g Poly, 3.5 g Sat); 19 mg Cholesterol; 18 g Carbohydrate; 2 g Fibre; 12 g Protein; 732 mg Sodium

Pictured on page 144.

Swiss Chard And Coconut Soup

A nice change from the ordinary!

Cooking oil	1 tbsp.	15 mL
Chopped onion	1 cup	250 mL
Garam masala	2 tsp.	10 mL
Garlic clove, minced (or 1/4 tsp., 1 mL, powder)	1	1
Chili powder	1 tsp.	5 mL
Prepared vegetable (or chicken) broth	3 – 4 cups	750 mL – 1 L
Chopped carrot	1 cup	250 mL
Chopped potato	1 cup	250 mL
Sliced mushrooms	1 cup	250 mL
Tomato paste	1/4 cup	60 mL
Chopped Swiss chard leaves	4 cups	1 L
Fresh (or frozen) peas	1 1/2 cups	375 mL
Can of coconut milk	14 oz.	398 mL
Salt	1/2 tsp.	2 mL

Heat cooking oil in large pot or Dutch oven on medium-low. Add next 4 ingredients. Cook for about 10 minutes, stirring occasionally, until onion is soft.

Add next 5 ingredients. Stir. Bring to a boil. Reduce heat to medium. Simmer, uncovered, for about 15 minutes until vegetables are tender.

Add remaining 4 ingredients. Heat and stir for 5 to 7 minutes until chard is wilted and mixture is very hot, but not boiling. Makes about 8 cups (2 L).

1 cup (250 mL): 194 Calories; 12.9 g Total Fat (1.7 g Mono, 0.9 g Poly, 9.3 g Sat); 0 mg Cholesterol; 16 g Carbohydrate; 2 g Fibre; 6 g Protein; 521 mg Sodium

Potato And Broccoli Soup

This soup will warm you from the inside out! Broccoli and Cheddar cheese
combine with a smooth potato base to make a very tasty blend.

Broccoli florets	4 cups	1 L
Water		
Hard margarine (or butter)	2 tbsp.	30 mL
Finely chopped leek (white and tender parts only)	1 1/2 cups	375 mL
All-purpose flour	2 tbsp.	30 mL
Prepared chicken broth	3 cups	750 mL
Milk	3 cups	750 mL
Dijon mustard	1 tbsp.	15 mL
Chopped potato	2 cups	500 mL
Grated medium Cheddar cheese	3/4 cup	175 mL
Pepper	1/4 tsp.	1 mL

Cook broccoli in water in large saucepan for about 5 minutes until tender.
Drain. Set aside.

Melt margarine in large pot or Dutch oven on medium-low. Add leek.
Cook for about 10 minutes, stirring occasionally, until tender.

Add flour. Heat and stir for about 1 minute until smooth.

Add broth, milk and mustard. Heat and stir on medium-high for 5 to
10 minutes until boiling and thickened.

Add potato. Stir. Cook, uncovered, on medium for about 15 minutes until
potato is tender. Cool slightly. Process potato mixture and 1/2 of broccoli
in blender until smooth. Return to pot. Chop remaining broccoli. Add to
potato mixture.

Add cheese and pepper. Heat and stir on medium for about 5 minutes until
cheese is melted and mixture is hot. Makes about 7 cups (1.75 L).

1 cup (250 mL): 221 Calories; 9.8 g Total Fat (4 g Mono, 0.9 g Poly, 4.4 g Sat); 18 mg Cholesterol;
22 g Carbohydrate; 3 g Fibre; 12 g Protein; 577 mg Sodium

Curried Zucchini Soup

This pale yellow soup has a wonderful hearty texture.
The mild curry and cauliflower flavours are evident.

Cooking oil	1 tbsp.	15 mL
Chopped onion	1 1/2 cups	375 mL
Garlic cloves, minced (or 1/2 tsp., 2 mL, powder)	2	2
Brown sugar, packed	1 tbsp.	15 mL
Lemon juice	1 tbsp.	15 mL
Mild curry paste	2 tbsp.	30 mL
Prepared chicken broth	4 cups	1 L
Cauliflower florets	2 cups	500 mL
Salt	1/4 – 1/2 tsp.	1 – 2 mL
Pepper	1/8 tsp.	0.5 mL
Chopped zucchini (with peel)	3 cups	750 mL
Whipping cream (or milk)	1 cup	250 mL
Chopped fresh parsley (or 1 1/2 tsp., 7 mL, flakes)	2 tbsp.	30 mL

Heat cooking oil in large pot or Dutch oven on medium. Add onion and garlic. Cook for about 20 minutes, stirring occasionally, until onion is very soft and golden.

Add brown sugar and lemon juice. Heat and stir until sugar is dissolved.

Add curry paste. Heat and stir for 1 to 2 minutes until fragrant.

Add next 4 ingredients. Stir. Bring to a boil. Reduce heat to medium. Simmer, uncovered, for 20 minutes.

Add zucchini. Stir. Cook for about 10 minutes until tender. Cool slightly. Process in blender, in 2 batches, until smooth. Return to pot.

Add whipping cream. Heat and stir on medium until very hot, but not boiling.

Add parsley. Stir. Makes about 6 cups (1.5 L).

1 cup (250 mL): 240 Calories; 18.8 g Total Fat (6.7 g Mono, 1.8 g Poly, 9 g Sat); 49 mg Cholesterol; 13 g Carbohydrate; 3 g Fibre; 7 g Protein; 677 mg Sodium

Measurement Tables

Throughout this book measurements are given in Conventional and Metric measure. To compensate for differences between the two measurements due to rounding, a full metric measure is not always used. The cup used is the standard 8 fluid ounce. Temperature is given in degrees Fahrenheit and Celsius. Baking pan measurements are in inches and centimetres as well as quarts and litres. An exact metric conversion is given below as well as the working equivalent (Metric Standard Measure).

Spoons

Conventional Measure	Metric Exact Conversion Millilitre (mL)	Metric Standard Measure Millilitre (mL)
1/8 teaspoon (tsp.)	0.6 mL	0.5 mL
1/4 teaspoon (tsp.)	1.2 mL	1 mL
1/2 teaspoon (tsp.)	2.4 mL	2 mL
1 teaspoon (tsp.)	4.7 mL	5 mL
2 teaspoons (tsp.)	9.4 mL	10 mL
1 tablespoon (tbsp.)	14.2 mL	15 mL

Cups

Conventional Measure	Metric Exact Conversion Millilitre (mL)	Metric Standard Measure Millilitre (mL)
1/4 cup (4 tbsp.)	56.8 mL	60 mL
1/3 cup (5 1/3 tbsp.)	75.6 mL	75 mL
1/2 cup (8 tbsp.)	113.7 mL	125 mL
2/3 cup (10 2/3 tbsp.)	151.2 mL	150 mL
3/4 cup (12 tbsp.)	170.5 mL	175 mL
1 cup (16 tbsp.)	227.3 mL	250 mL
4 1/2 cups	1022.9 mL	1000 mL (1 L)

Oven Temperatures

Fahrenheit (°F)	Celsius (°C)
175°	80°
200°	95°
225°	110°
250°	120°
275°	140°
300°	150°
325°	160°
350°	175°
375°	190°
400°	205°
425°	220°
450°	230°
475°	240°
500°	260°

Dry Measurements

Conventional Measure Ounces (oz.)	Metric Exact Conversion Grams (g)	Metric Standard Measure Grams (g)
1 oz.	28.3 g	28 g
2 oz.	56.7 g	57 g
3 oz.	85.0 g	85 g
4 oz.	113.4 g	125 g
5 oz.	141.7 g	140 g
6 oz.	170.1 g	170 g
7 oz.	198.4 g	200 g
8 oz.	226.8 g	250 g
16 oz.	453.6 g	500 g
32 oz.	907.2 g	1000 g (1 kg)

Pans

Conventional Inches	Metric Centimetres
8x8 inch	20x20 cm
9x9 inch	22x22 cm
9x13 inch	22x33 cm
10x15 inch	25x38 cm
11x17 inch	28x43 cm
8x2 inch round	20x5 cm
9x2 inch round	22x5 cm
10x4 1/2 inch tube	25x11 cm
8x4x3 inch loaf	20x10x7.5 cm
9x5x3 inch loaf	22x12.5x7.5 cm

Casseroles

CANADA & BRITAIN Standard Size Casserole	Exact Metric Measure	UNITED STATES Standard Size Casserole	Exact Metric Measure
1 qt. (5 cups)	1.13 L	1 qt. (4 cups)	900 mL
1 1/2 qts. (7 1/2 cups)	1.69 L	1 1/2 qts. (6 cups)	1.35 L
2 qts. (10 cups)	2.25 L	2 qts. (8 cups)	1.8 L
2 1/2 qts. (12 1/2 cups)	2.81 L	2 1/2 qts. (10 cups)	2.25 L
3 qts. (15 cups)	3.38 L	3 qts. (12 cups)	2.7 L
4 qts. (20 cups)	4.5 L	4 qts. (16 cups)	3.6 L
5 qts. (25 cups)	5.63 L	5 qts. (20 cups)	4.5 L

Tip Index

151

Recipe Index

153

154

155

Company's Coming cookbooks are available at retail locations throughout Canada!

EXCLUSIVE mail order offer on next page
Buy any 2 cookbooks—choose a 3rd FREE of equal or less value than the lowest price paid.

Original Series   CA$14.99 Canada   US$10.99 USA & International

CODE		CODE		CODE	
SQ	150 Delicious Squares	KC	Kids Cooking	FD	Fondues
CA	Casseroles	CT	Cooking For Two	CCBE	The Beef Book
MU	Muffins & More	BB	Breakfasts & Brunches	ASI	Asian Cooking
SA	Salads	SC	Slow Cooker Recipes	CB	The Cheese Book
AP	Appetizers	ODM	One-Dish Meals	RC	The Rookie Cook
DE	Desserts	ST	Starters	RHR	Rush-Hour Recipes
SS	Soups & Sandwiches	SF	Stir-Fry	SW	Sweet Cravings
CO	Cookies	MAM	Make-Ahead Meals	YRG	Year-Round Grilling
PA	Pasta	PB	The Potato Book	GG	Garden Greens
BA	Barbecues	CCLFC	Low-Fat Cooking	CHC	Chinese Cooking **NEW** Aug 1/03
LR	Light Recipes	CCLFP	Low-Fat Pasta		
PR	Preserves	CFK	Cook For Kids		
CH	Chicken, Etc.	SCH	Stews, Chilies & Chowders		

Greatest Hits Series

CODE	CA$12.99 Canada US$9.99 USA & International
ITAL	Italian
MEX	Mexican

Lifestyle Series

CODE	CA$16.99 Canada US$12.99 USA & International
GR	Grilling
DC	Diabetic Cooking

CODE	CA$19.99 Canada US$17.99 USA & International
HC	Heart-Friendly Cooking

Special Occasion Series

CODE	CA$19.99 Canada US$17.99 USA & International
GFK	Gifts from the Kitchen
CFS	Cooking for the Seasons

CODE	CA$22.99 Canada US$17.99 USA & International
WC	Weekend Cooking

CODE	CA$24.99 Canada US$19.99 USA & International
HFH	Home for the Holidays

Company's Coming
COOKBOOKS®

COMPANY'S COMING PUBLISHING LIMITED
2311 – 96 Street
Edmonton, Alberta, Canada T6N 1G3
Tel: (780) 450-6223   Fax: (780) 450-1857
www.companyscoming.com

EXCLUSIVE Mail Order Offer
See previous page for list of cookbooks

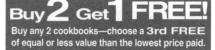

Buy 2 Get 1 FREE!
Buy any 2 cookbooks—choose a **3rd FREE**
of equal or less value than the lowest price paid.

Quantity	Code	Title	Price Each	Price Total
			$	$
		DON'T FORGET to indicate your FREE BOOK(S). (see exclusive mail order offer above) please print		
	TOTAL BOOKS (including FREE)	**TOTAL BOOKS PURCHASED:**	$	

	International		Canada & USA	
Plus Shipping & Handling (per destination)	$7.00	(one book)	$5.00	(1-3 books)
Additional Books (including FREE books)	$	($2.00 each)	$	($1.00 each)
Sub-Total	$		$	
Canadian residents add G.S.T(7%)			$	
TOTAL AMOUNT ENCLOSED	$		$	

The Fine Print

- Orders outside Canada must be **PAID IN US FUNDS** by cheque or money order drawn on Canadian or US bank or by credit card.
- Make cheque or money order payable to: **COMPANY'S COMING PUBLISHING LIMITED.**
- Prices are expressed in Canadian dollars for Canada, US dollars for USA & International and are subject to change without prior notice.
- Orders are shipped surface mail. For courier rates, visit our web-site: **companyscoming.com** or contact us:
  Tel: (780) 450-6223 Fax: (780) 450-1857.
- Sorry, no C.O.D's.

Gift Giving

- Let us help you with your gift giving!
- We will send cookbooks directly to the recipients of your choice if you give us their names and addresses.
- Please specify the titles you wish to send to each person.
- If you would like to include your personal note or card, we will be pleased to enclose it with your gift order.

158

☐ MasterCard. ☐ VISA _____
Expiry date

Account # _____

Name of cardholder _____

Cardholder's signature _____

Shipping Address
Send the cookbooks listed above to:

Name: _____

Street: _____

City: _____ Prov./State: ____

Country: _____ Postal Code/Zip: ___

Tel: (_____) _____

E-mail address: _____

☐ YES! Please send a catalogue

COOKBOOKS

The weekend is finally here—time to relax with family, friends and plenty of good food! Keep the festivities rolling with your choice of casual entertaining ideas from *Weekend Cooking*.

Inside you'll find 40 creative menu plans featuring more than 200 all-new, kitchen-tested recipes. *Weekend Cooking* features everything from a laid-back video night of snacking to an exotic African safari party to a spicy Australian barbecue. Each recipe has been beautifully photographed and is easy to follow, for winning results every time.

Whenever family and friends come together on the weekend, save time to enjoy their company. Count on *Weekend Cooking* for your menu plan!

Quick
&
Easy
Recipes

Everyday
Ingredients

Canada's
most popular
cookbooks!

Complete your Original Series Collection!

- ❑ 150 Delicious Squares
- ❑ Casseroles
- ❑ Muffins & More
- ❑ Salads
- ❑ Appetizers
- ❑ Desserts
- ❑ Soups & Sandwiches
- ❑ Cookies
- ❑ Pasta
- ❑ Barbecues
- ❑ Light Recipes
- ❑ Preserves
- ❑ Chicken, Etc.
- ❑ Kids Cooking
- ❑ Cooking For Two
- ❑ Breakfasts & Brunches
- ❑ Slow Cooker Recipes
- ❑ One-Dish Meals
- ❑ Starters
- ❑ Stir-Fry
- ❑ Make-Ahead Meals
- ❑ The Potato Book
- ❑ Low-Fat Cooking
- ❑ Low-Fat Pasta
- ❑ Cook For Kids
- ❑ Stews, Chilies & Chowders
- ❑ Fondues
- ❑ The Beef Book
- ❑ Asian Cooking
- ❑ The Cheese Book
- ❑ The Rookie Cook
- ❑ Rush-Hour Recipes
- ❑ Sweet Cravings
- ❑ Year-Round Grilling
- ❑ Garden Greens
- ❑ Chinese Cooking **NEW** Aug 1/03

COLLECT ALL Company's Coming Series Cookbooks!

Greatest Hits Series

- ❑ Italian
- ❑ Mexican

Special Occasion Series

- ❑ Gifts from the Kitchen
- ❑ Cooking for the Seasons
- ❑ Home for the Holidays
- ❑ Weekend Cooking

Lifestyle Series

- ❑ Grilling
- ❑ Diabetic Cooking
- ❑ Heart-Friendly Cooking

Canada's most popular cookbooks!